THIRD EDITION

3B

Skills for Success
READING AND WRITING

Colin S. Ward | Margot F. Gramer

OXFORD
UNIVERSITY PRESS

198 Madison Avenue
New York, NY 10016 USA

Great Clarendon Street, Oxford, OX2 6DP, United Kingdom

Oxford University Press is a department of the University of Oxford. It furthers the University's objective of excellence in research, scholarship, and education by publishing worldwide. Oxford is a registered trade mark of Oxford University Press in the UK and in certain other countries

© Oxford University Press 2019

The moral rights of the author have been asserted

First published in 2019

2023 2022 2021 2020 2019
10 9 8 7 6 5 4 3 2 1

No unauthorized photocopying

All rights reserved. No part of this publication may be reproduced, stored in a retrieval system, or transmitted, in any form or by any means, without the prior permission in writing of Oxford University Press, or as expressly permitted by law, by licence or under terms agreed with the appropriate reprographics rights organization. Enquiries concerning reproduction outside the scope of the above should be sent to the ELT Rights Department, Oxford University Press, at the address above

You must not circulate this work in any other form and you must impose this same condition on any acquirer

Links to third party websites are provided by Oxford in good faith and for information only. Oxford disclaims any responsibility for the materials contained in any third party website referenced in this work

ISBN: 978 0 19 490412 4   Student Book 3B with iQ Online pack
ISBN: 978 0 19 490382 0   Student Book 3B as pack component
ISBN: 978 0 19 490430 8   iQ Online student website

Printed in China

This book is printed on paper from certified and well-managed sources

ACKNOWLEDGEMENTS

Back cover photograph: Oxford University Press building/David Fisher
Illustrations by: Karen Minot p.32

The Publishers would like to thank the following for their kind permission to reproduce photographs and other copyright material:

Alamy: pp.27 (woman presenting to colleagues/Hero Images Inc.), 43 (Chinese restaurant/Edward Herdwick), 73 (man crossing road/SiliconValleyStock), 80 (Times Square/Alexander Spatari), 84 (woman shopping/Phanie), 95 (social media login page/LondonPhotos - Homer Sykes), 112 (children in front of shack/imagebroker), 185 (woman weaving basket/Jake Lyell); Getty: Cover (Alfon No/500px Prime), pp.2 (man presenting to group/Caiaimage/TomMerton), 5 (small talk/Caiaimage/Paul Bradbury), 6 (businessmen shaking hands/Caiaimage/Paul Bradbury), 18 (family greeting/Hero Images), 28 (chef plating up food/Carlos Sanchez Pereyra), 31 (woman pulling sour face/Eva-Katalin), 54 (girl in basket with cellphone/Bloomberg), 58 (driverless car/Chesky_W), 64 (children working on tablets/PeopleImages), 83 (couple in a restaurant/10'000 Hours), 88 (bus advertisement/Richard Baker / Contributor), 104 (man running with prosthetic/MichaelSvoboda), 107 (girl being introduced to class/Niedring/Drentwett), 108 (man in front of devastated house/David DUCOIN / Contributor), 130 (boy choosing a skateboard/Sigrid Gombert), 136 (students running up steps/XiXinXing), 145 (business people around a table/Thomas Barwick), 157 (mother and daughter choosing cakes/Hero Images), 162 (FEED bags/Astrid Stawiarz / Stringer), 173 (group of people with plant saplings/PeopleImages), 186 (women celebrating ascent of mountain/swissmediavision), 210 (football team celebrating success/Hero Images); OUP: pp.65 (façade of Petra/Shutterstock/Yongyut Kumsri), 103 (hot air balloons/Shutterstock / Twin Design), 134 (student thinking/wavebreakmedia), 146 (firefighters tackling a blaze/Shutterstock/Johnny Habell), 175 (black rhino/Shutterstock/AndChisPhoto), 194 (woman running/Shutterstock/Daxiao Productions); Shutterstock: pp.13 (video conference/fizkes), 16 (woman in job interview/Lucky Business), 38 (attractive dish of food/Ricardo Villasenor), 39 (dessert on plate/Andreshkova Nastya), 53 (food hall in Thailand/Steve Allen), 57 (man in driverless car/Scharfsinn), 65 (POV taking photo on cellphone/tanatat), 69 (buying online with credit card/Worawee Meepian), 79 (airport checkin kiosks/i viewfinder), 84 (hiking boot/Cultura Motion), 90 (woman in café/ShutterOK), 116 (climbers on Half Dome mountain/Mark Yarchoan), 117 (Half Dome/klarka0608), 120 (person on galloping horse/NiP STUDIO), 129 (people repairing a damaged roof/Str/EPA), 133 (people waiting for elevator/Dragon Images), 180 (sunflower in field/Matt Kremkau), 189 (F1 car/Jens Mommens), 190 (F1 driver/cristiano barni), 195 (young boys playing soccer/Fotokostic), 199 (university football team/Keeton Gale), 201 (boys playing soccer in playground/sunsinger); Third party: pp.84 (Adchoice logo/Adchoice), 158 (eyeglasses being fitted to man/VisionSpring@Bangladesh), 161 (Lauren Bush Lauren handing out a school meal/FEED Projects), 168 (children wearing TOMS shoes/TOMS shoes), 169 (children with Nokero lights/Nokero Solar), 171 (woman fitting girl with shoe/TOMS shoes).

The authors and publisher are grateful to those who have given permission to reproduce the following extracts and adaptations of copyright material:

p. 90 From 'In Defense of Advertising' by Terry O'Reilly and Mike Tennant, from The Age of Persuasion Radio Show, CBC radio, broadcast April 26, 2008, www.cbc.ca. Reproduced by permission.

p. 107 From 'How People Learn to Become Resilient' by Maria Konnikova, 11 February, 2016. The New Yorker © Condé Nast. Reproduced by permission.

p. 116 Extract from 'The Climb of My Life: Scaling Mountains with a Borrowed Heart' by Kelly Perkins, 2007, Rowman and Littlefield Publishers. Reproduced by permission of Kelly Perkins.

Although every effort has been made to trace and contact copyright holders before publication, this has not been possible in some cases. We apologize for any apparent infringement of copyright and if notified, the publisher will be pleased to rectify any errors or omissions at the earliest opportunity.

Sources: p. 161 www.forbes.com, www.feedprojects.com

ACKNOWLEDGMENTS

We would like to acknowledge the teachers from all over the world who participated in the development process and review of *Q: Skills for Success* Third Edition.

USA

Kate Austin, Avila University, MO; **Sydney Bassett**, Auburn Global University, AL; **Michael Beamer**, USC, CA; **Renae Betten**, CBU, CA; **Pepper Boyer**, Auburn Global University, AL; **Marina Broeder**, Mission College, CA; **Thomas Brynmore**, Auburn Global University, AL; **Britta Burton**, Mission College, CA; **Kathleen Castello**, Mission College, CA; **Teresa Cheung**, North Shore Community College, MA; **Shantall Colebrooke**, Auburn Global University, AL; **Kyle Cooper**, Troy University, AL; **Elizabeth Cox**, Auburn Global University, AL; **Ashley Ekers**, Auburn Global University, AL; **Rhonda Farley**, Los Rios Community College, CA; **Marcus Frame**, Troy University, AL; **Lora Glaser**, Mission College, CA; **Hala Hamka**, Henry Ford College, MI; **Shelley A. Harrington**, Henry Ford College, MI; **Barrett J. Heusch**, Troy University, AL; **Beth Hill**, St. Charles Community College, MO; **Patty Jones**, Troy University, AL; **Tom Justice**, North Shore Community College, MA; **Robert Klein**, Troy University, AL; **Patrick Maestas**, Auburn Global University, AL; **Elizabeth Merchant**, Auburn Global University, AL; **Rosemary Miketa**, Henry Ford College, MI; **Myo Myint**, Mission College, CA; **Lance Noe**, Troy University, AL; **Irene Pannatier**, Auburn Global University, AL; **Annie Percy**, Troy University, AL; **Erin Robinson**, Troy University, AL; **Juliane Rosner**, Mission College, CA; **Mary Stevens**, North Shore Community College, MA; **Pamela Stewart**, Henry Ford College, MI; **Karen Tucker**, Georgia Tech, GA; **Loreley Wheeler**, North Shore Community College, MA; **Amanda Wilcox**, Auburn Global University, AL; **Heike Williams**, Auburn Global University, AL

Canada

Angelika Brunel, Collège Ahuntsic, QC; **David Butler**, English Language Institute, BC; **Paul Edwards**, Kwantlen Polytechnic University, BC; **Cody Hawver**, University of British Columbia, BC; **Olivera Jovovic**, Kwantlen Polytechnic University, BC; **Tami Moffatt**, University of British Columbia, BC; **Dana Pynn**, Vancouver Island University, BC

Latin America

Georgette Barreda, SENATI, Peru; **Claudia Cecilia Díaz Romero**, Colegio América, Mexico; **Jeferson Ferro**, Uninter, Brazil; **Mayda Hernández**, English Center, Mexico; **Jose Ixtaccihusatl**, Instituto Tecnológico de Tecomatlán, Mexico; **Andreas Paulus Pabst**, CBA Idiomas, Brazil; **Amanda Carla Pas**, Instituição de Ensino Santa Izildinha, Brazil; **Allen Quesada Pacheco**, University of Costa Rica, Costa Rica; **Rolando Sánchez**, Escuela Normal de Tecámac, Mexico; **Luis Vasquez**, CESNO, Mexico

Asia

Asami Atsuko, Women's University, Japan; **Rene Bouchard**, Chinzei Keiai Gakuen, Japan; **Francis Brannen**, Sangmyung University, South Korea; **Haeyun Cho**, Sogang University, South Korea; **Daniel Craig**, Sangmyung University, South Korea; **Thomas Cuming**, Royal Melbourne Institute of Technology, Vietnam; **Jissen Joshi Daigaku**, Women's University, Japan; **Nguyen Duc Dat**, OISP, Vietnam; **Wayne Devitte**, Tokai University, Japan; **James D. Dunn**, Tokai University, Japan; **Fergus Hann**, Tokai University, Japan; **Michael Hood**, Nihon University College of Commerce, Japan; **Hideyuki Kashimoto**, Shijonawate High School, Japan; **David Kennedy**, Nihon University, Japan; **Anna Youngna Kim**, Sogang University, South Korea; **Jae Phil Kim**, Sogang University, South Korea; **Jaganathan Krishnasamy**, GB Academy, Malaysia; **Peter Laver**, Incheon National University, South Korea; **Hung Hoang Le**, Ho Chi Minh City University of Technology, Vietnam; **Hyon Sook Lee**, Sogang University, South Korea; **Ji-seon Lee**, Iruda English Institute, South Korea; **Joo Young Lee**, Sogang University, South Korea; **Phung Tu Luc**, Ho Chi Minh City University of Technology, Vietnam; **Richard Mansbridge**, Hoa Sen University, Vietnam; **Kahoko Matsumoto**, Tokai University, Japan; **Elizabeth May**, Sangmyung University, South Korea; **Naoyuki Naganuma**, Tokai University, Japan; **Hiroko Nishikage**, Taisho University, Japan; **Yongjun Park**, Sangji University, South Korea; **Paul Rogers**, Dongguk University, South Korea; **Scott Schafer**, Inha University, South Korea; **Michael Schvaudner**, Tokai University, Japan; **Brendan Smith**, RMIT University, School of Languages and English, Vietnam; **Peter Snashall**, Huachiew Chalermprakiet University, Thailand; Makoto Takeda, Sendai Third Senior High School, Japan; **Peter Talley**, Mahidol University, Faculty of ICT, Thailand; **Byron Thigpen**, Sogang University, South Korea; **Junko Yamaai**, Tokai University, Japan; **Junji Yamada**, Taisho University, Japan; **Sayoko Yamashita**, Women's University, Japan; **Masami Yukimori**, Taisho University, Japan

Middle East and North Africa

Sajjad Ahmad, Taibah University, Saudi Arabia; **Basma Alansari**, Taibah University, Saudi Arabia; **Marwa Al-ashqar**, Taibah University, Saudi Arabia; **Dr. Rashid Al-Khawaldeh**, Taibah University, Saudi Arabia; **Mohamed Almohamed**, Taibah University, Saudi Arabia; **Dr Musaad Alrahaili**, Taibah University, Saudi Arabia; **Hala Al Sammar**, Kuwait University, Kuwait; **Ahmed Alshammari**, Taibah University, Saudi Arabia; **Ahmed Alshamy**, Taibah University, Saudi Arabia; **Doniazad sultan AlShraideh**, Taibah University, Saudi Arabia; **Sahar Amer**, Taibah University, Saudi Arabia; **Nabeela Azam**, Taibah University, Saudi Arabia; **Hassan Bashir, Edex**, Saudi Arabia; **Rachel Batchilder**, College of the North Atlantic, Qatar; **Nicole Cuddie**, Community College of Qatar, Qatar; **Mahdi Duris**, King Saud University, Saudi Arabia; **Ahmed Ege**, Institute of Public Administration, Saudi Arabia; **Magda Fadle**, Victoria College, Egypt; **Mohammed Hassan**, Taibah University, Saudi Arabia; **Tom Hodgson**, Community College of Qatar, Qatar; **Ayub Agbar Khan**, Taibah University, Saudi Arabia; **Cynthia Le Joncour**, Taibah University, Saudi Arabia; **Ruari Alexander MacLeod**, Community College of Qatar, Qatar; **Nasir Mahmood**, Taibah University, Saudi Arabia; **Duria Salih Mahmoud**, Taibah University, Saudi Arabia; **Ameera McKoy**, Taibah University, Saudi Arabia; **Chaker Mhamdi**, Buraimi University College, Oman; **Baraa Shiekh Mohamed**, Community College of Qatar, Qatar; **Abduleelah Mohammed**, Taibah University, Saudi Arabia; **Shumaila Nasir**, Taibah University, Saudi Arabia; Kevin Onwordi, Taibah University, Saudi Arabia; **Dr. Navid Rahmani**, Community College of Qatar, Qatar; **Dr. Sabah Salman Sabbah**, Community College of Qatar, Qatar; **Salih**, Taibah University, Saudi Arabia; **Verna Santos-Nafrada**, King Saud University, Saudi Arabia; **Gamal Abdelfattah Shehata**, Taibah University, Saudi Arabia; **Ron Stefan**, Institute of Public Administration, Saudi Arabia; **Dr. Saad Torki**, Imam Abdulrahman Bin Faisal University, Dammam, Saudi Arabia; **Silvia Yafai**, Applied Technology High School/Secondary Technical School, UAE; **Mahmood Zar**, Taibah University, Saudi Arabia; **Thouraya Zheni**, Taibah University, Saudi Arabia

Turkey

Sema Babacan, Istanbul Medipol University; **Bilge Çöllüoğlu Yakar**, Bilkent University; **Liana Corniel**, Koc University; **Savas Geylanioglu**, Izmir Bahcesehir Science and Technology College; **Öznur Güler**, Giresun University; **Selen Bilginer Halefoğlu**, Maltepe University; **Ahmet Konukoğlu**, Hasan Kalyoncu University; **Mehmet Salih Yoğun**, Gaziantep Hasan Kalyoncu University; **Fatih Yücel**, Beykent University

Europe

Amina Al Hashamia, University of Exeter, UK; **Irina Gerasimova**, Saint-Petersburg Mining University, Russia; **Jodi**, Las Dominicas, Spain; **Marina Khanykova**, School 179, Russia; **Oksana Postnikova**, Lingua Practica, Russia; **Nina Vasilchenko**, Soho-Bridge Language School, Russia

Q: Skills For Success THIRD EDITION

CRITICAL THINKING

The unique critical thinking approach of the *Q: Skills for Success* series has been further enhanced in the Third Edition. New features help you analyze, synthesize, and develop your ideas.

Unit question
The thought-provoking unit questions engage you with the topic and provide a critical thinking framework for the unit.

> **UNIT QUESTION**
> **How do you make a good first impression?**
>
> **A. Discuss these questions with your classmates.**
> 1. What qualities do you look for in a friend?
> 2. What is the best way to make a good first impression on a classmate? On a boss?
> 3. Look at the photo. Describe the people in the room. Where are they? What is the man standing up doing?
>
> **B.** Listen to *The Q Classroom* online. Then complete the chart with the suggestions from the box.

Analysis
You can discuss your opinion of each reading text and analyze how it changes your perspective on the unit question.

> **G. DISCUSS** Work with a partner. Make a list of decisions you made today. Which ones do you think were lazy? Which ones were not lazy?
>
> **iQ PRACTICE** Go online for additional reading and comprehension. *Practice > Unit 6 > Activity 4*
>
> **WRITE WHAT YOU THINK**
>
> **A. DISCUSS** Discuss the questions in a group. Think about the Unit Question, "Are you a good decision maker?"
> 1. Do you think you are a lazy thinker when you make decisions? Why or why not?
> 2. When did you make a decision using hard thinking? Was it a good decision?
> 3. When you meet someone new, can you tell if the person is honest or not? How?
>
> **B. COMPOSE** Choose one of the questions from Activity A and write a paragraph in response. Look back at your Quick Write on page 132 as you think about what you learned.

NEW! Critical Thinking Strategy with video
Each unit includes a Critical Thinking Strategy with activities to give you step-by-step guidance in critical analysis of texts. An accompanying instructional video (available on iQ Online) provides extra support and examples.

NEW! Bloom's Taxonomy
Blue activity headings integrate verbs from Bloom's Taxonomy to help you see how each activity develops critical thinking skills.

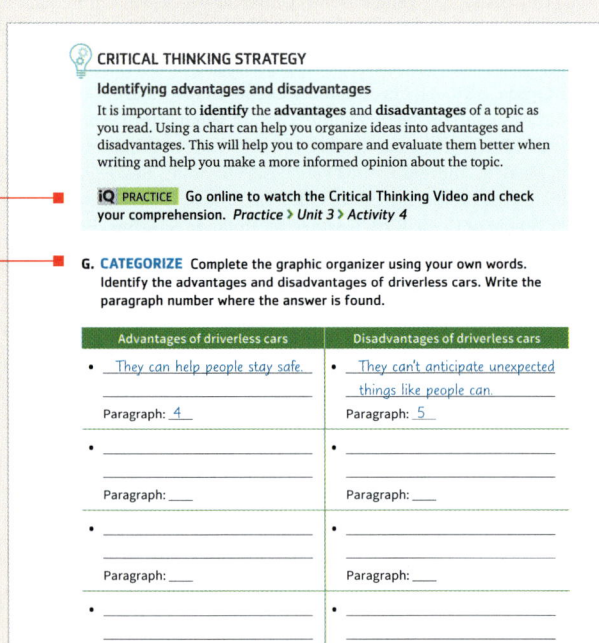

> **CRITICAL THINKING STRATEGY**
>
> **Identifying advantages and disadvantages**
> It is important to **identify** the **advantages** and **disadvantages** of a topic as you read. Using a chart can help you organize ideas into advantages and disadvantages. This will help you to compare and evaluate them better when writing and help you make a more informed opinion about the topic.
>
> **iQ PRACTICE** Go online to watch the Critical Thinking Video and check your comprehension. *Practice > Unit 3 > Activity 4*
>
> **G. CATEGORIZE** Complete the graphic organizer using your own words. Identify the advantages and disadvantages of driverless cars. Write the paragraph number where the answer is found.
>
> | Advantages of driverless cars | Disadvantages of driverless cars |
> |---|---|
> | They can help people stay safe. Paragraph: 4 | They can't anticipate unexpected things like people can. Paragraph: 5 |
> | Paragraph: ___ | Paragraph: ___ |
> | Paragraph: ___ | Paragraph: ___ |
> | Paragraph: ___ | Paragraph: ___ |
>
> **H. DISCUSS** Work with a partner. Discuss how the advantages and disadvantages of driverless cars would affect transportation in the future.
>
> **iQ PRACTICE** Go online for additional reading and comprehension. *Practice > Unit 3 > Activity 5*

THREE TYPES OF VIDEO

UNIT VIDEO

The unit videos include high-interest documentaries and reports on a wide variety of subjects, all linked to the unit topic and question.

NEW! "Work with the Video" pages guide you in watching, understanding, and discussing the unit videos. The activities help you see the connection to the Unit Question and the other texts in the unit.

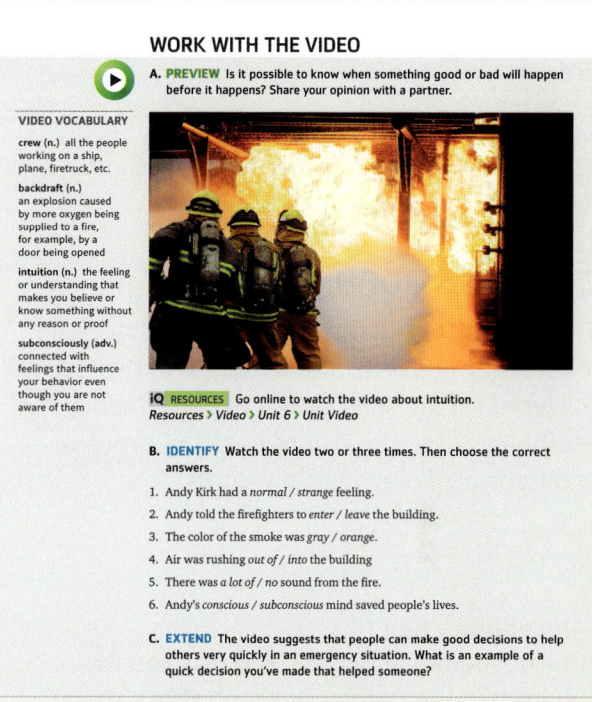

CRITICAL THINKING VIDEO

NEW! Narrated by the Q series authors, these short videos give you further instruction into the Critical Thinking Strategy of each unit using engaging images and graphics. You can use them to get a deeper understanding of the Critical Thinking Strategy.

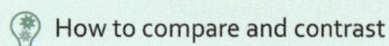

SKILLS VIDEO

NEW! These instructional videos provide illustrated explanations of skills and grammar points in the Student Book. They can be viewed in class or assigned for a flipped classroom, for homework, or for review. One skill video is available for every unit.

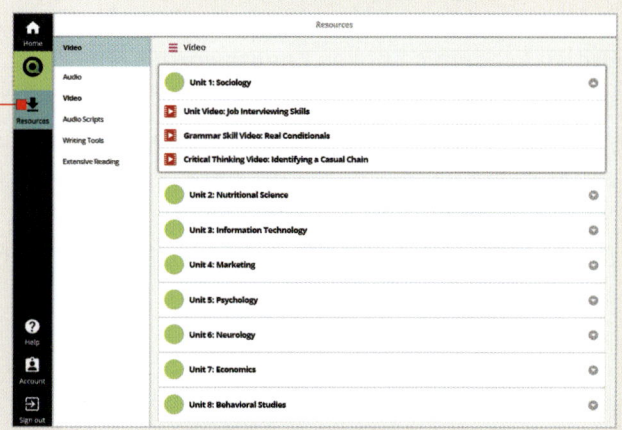

Easily access all videos in the Resources section of iQ Online.

VOCABULARY

A research-based vocabulary program focuses on the words you need to know academically and professionally.

The vocabulary syllabus in *Q: Skills for Success* is correlated to the CEFR (see page 212) and linked to two word lists: the Oxford 3000 and the OPAL (Oxford Phrasal Academic Lexicon).

OXFORD 3000

The Oxford 3000 lists the core words that every learner at the A1–B2 level needs to know. Items in the word list are selected for their frequency and usefulness from the Oxford English Corpus (a database of over 2 billion words).

Vocabulary Key
In vocabulary activities, 🔑 shows you the word is in the Oxford 3000 and **OPAL** shows you the word or phrase is in the OPAL.

- ☐ to explain the sport of Formula 1 car racing
- ☐ to encourage businesses to invest in car racing
- ☐ to compare Formula 1 car races around the world
- ☐ to show why car racing is an expensive sport

B. QUICK WRITE What are some ways businesses attract more customers? Write for 5–10 minutes in response. Be sure to use this section for your Unit Assignment.

C. VOCABULARY Check (✓) the words you know. Then work with a partner to locate each word in the reading. Use clues to help define the words you don't know. Check your definitions in the dictionary.

assured (adj.)	invest (v.) 🔑	profit (n.) 🔑
dependable (adj.)	logo (n.)	sponsor (v.) 🔑
expansion (n.) OPAL	market (n.) 🔑	stability (n.) OPAL
image (n.) 🔑 OPAL		

🔑 Oxford 3000™ words   **OPAL** Oxford Phrasal Academic Lexicon

iQ PRACTICE Go online to listen and practice your pronunciation.
Practice › Unit 8 › Activity 2

OPAL
OXFORD PHRASAL ACADEMIC LEXICON

NEW! The OPAL is a collection of four word lists that provide an essential guide to the most important words and phrases to know for academic English. The word lists are based on the Oxford Corpus of Academic English and the British Academic Spoken English corpus. The OPAL includes both spoken and written academic English and both individual words and longer phrases.

Academic Language tips in the Student Book give information about how words and phrases from the OPAL are used and offer help with features such as collocations and phrasal verbs.

ACADEMIC LANGUAGE
The corpus shows that **based on** is often used in academic writing.
Based on the results . . .
. . . the research was based on . . .
OPAL Oxford Phrasal Academic Lexicon

3. Jack's question at the meeting was not _____ of low sales; it was completely off topic.

4. Sam recommended some articles on the effects of online a_____ These articles _____ his own views, based has done.

5. Mr. Santana needs to _____ that marketing profession for him. He needs to find another area that will skills better.

6. If you plan to study in a financial area such as accounting, sure that your work is always _____.

7. One _____ that has caused changes in adv popularity of social media.

8. People are constantly on their smartphones; this has had a _____ on how people communicate.

9. The students are looking at their phones. This _____ instructor that they are not interested in the class.

iQ PRACTICE Go online for more practice with the vocabul
Practice › Unit 4 › Activity 3

C. IDENTIFY Read the main ideas. Write the paragraph nu are found.

EXTENSIVE READING

NEW! Extensive Reading is a program of reading for pleasure at a level that matches your language ability.

There are many benefits to Extensive Reading:

- It helps you to become a better reader in general.
- It helps to increase your reading speed.
- It can improve your reading comprehension.
- It increases your vocabulary range.
- It can improve your grammar and writing skills.
- It's great for motivation—reading something that is interesting for its own sake.

Each unit of *Q: Skills for Success* Third Edition has been aligned to an Oxford Graded Reader based on the appropriate topic and level of language proficiency. The first chapter of each recommended graded reader can be downloaded from iQ Online Resources.

What is iQ ONLINE?

iQ ONLINE extends your learning beyond the classroom.

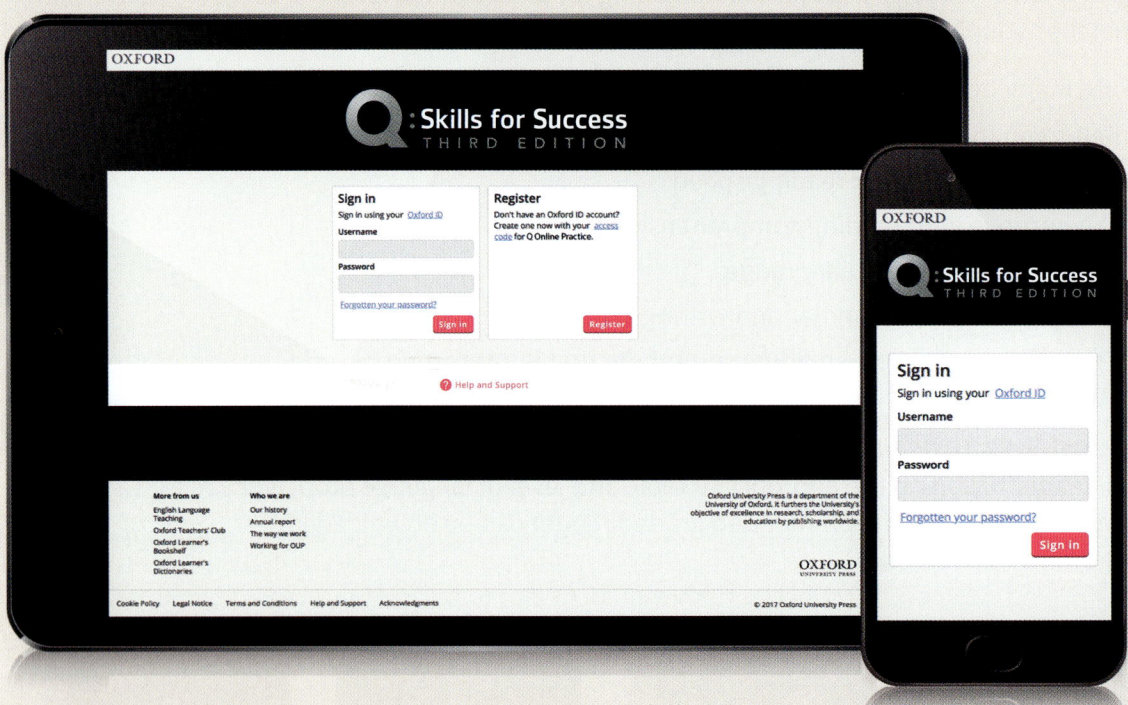

- Practice activities provide essential skills practice and support.
- Automatic grading and progress reports show you what you have mastered and where you need more practice.
- The Discussion Board allows you to discuss the Unit Questions and helps you develop your critical thinking.
- Essential resources such as audio and video are easy to access anytime.

NEW TO THE THIRD EDITION

- iQ Online is optimized for mobile use so you can use it on your phone.
- An updated interface allows easy navigation around the activities, tests, resources, and scores.
- New Critical Thinking Videos expand on the Critical Thinking Strategies in the Student Book.
- The Extensive Reading program helps you improve your vocabulary and reading skills.

How to use iQ ONLINE

Go to **Practice** to find additional practice and support to complement your learning in the classroom.

Go to **Resources** to find
- All Student Book video
- All Student Book audio
- Critical Thinking videos
- Skills videos
- Extensive Reading

Go to **Messages** and **Discussion Board** to communicate with your teacher and classmates.

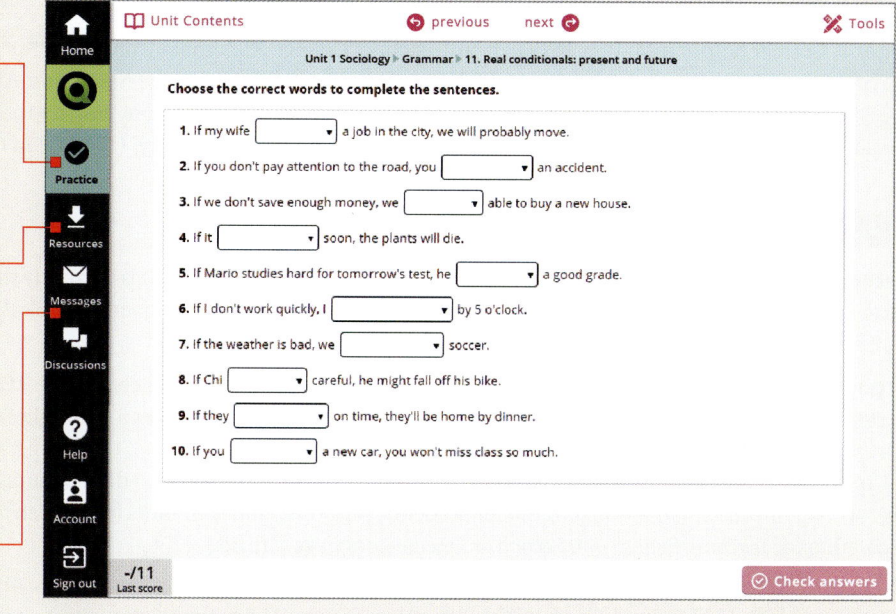

Online tests assigned by your teacher help you assess your progress and see where you still need more practice.

Progress bar shows you how many activities you have completed.

View your scores for all activities.

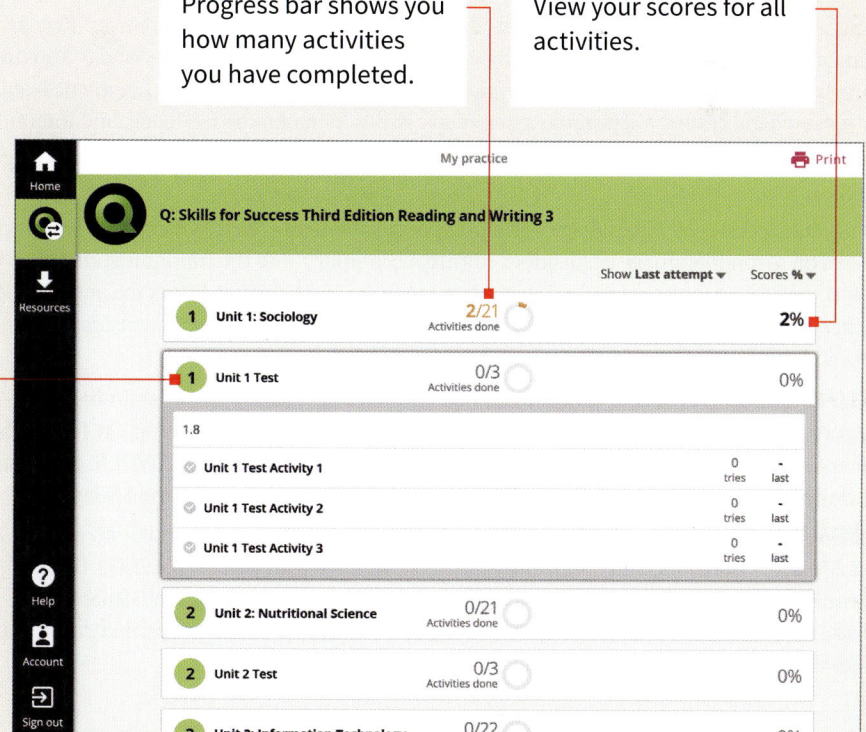

ix

AUTHORS AND CONSULTANTS

AUTHORS

Colin S. Ward is Chair of the Languages Department at Lone Star College-North Harris in Houston, Texas. He holds an M.A. in TESOL from the University of London and has been teaching English for over fifteen years. His interests include content-based language learning and the teaching of second-language writing. Colin is a U.S.-U.K. Fulbright scholar and the author of several ESL textbooks.

Margot F. Gramer holds an M.A. in TESOL from Teachers College, Columbia University. She has been involved in the field of ESL as a teacher, teacher-trainer, administrator, writer and editor. She has taught ESL for many years at both the college level and in business settings. She is the author or co-author of many ESL textbooks. She is currently an Instructor at the Language Immersion Program at Nassau Community College (LINCC) in Garden City, New York.

SERIES CONSULTANTS

Lawrence J. Zwier holds an M.A. in TESL from the University of Minnesota. He is currently the Associate Director for Curriculum Development at the English Language Center at Michigan State University in East Lansing. He has taught ESL/EFL in the United States, Saudi Arabia, Malaysia, Japan, and Singapore.

Marguerite Ann Snow holds a Ph.D. in Applied Linguistics from UCLA. She teaches in the TESOL M.A. program in the Charter College of Education at California State University, Los Angeles. She was a Fulbright scholar in Hong Kong and Cyprus. In 2006, she received the President's Distinguished Professor award at CSULA. She has trained ESL teachers in the United States and EFL teachers in more than 25 countries. She is the author/editor of numerous publications in the areas of content-based instruction, English for academic purposes, and standards for English teaching and learning. She is a co-editor of *Teaching English as a Second or Foreign Language* (4th ed.).

CRITICAL THINKING CONSULTANT **James Dunn** is a Junior Associate Professor at Tokai University and the Coordinator of the JALT Critical Thinking Special Interest Group. His research interests include critical thinking skills' impact on student brain function during English learning as measured by EEG. His educational goals are to help students understand that they are capable of more than they might think and to expand their cultural competence with critical thinking and higher-order thinking skills.

ASSESSMENT CONSULTANT **Elaine Boyd** has worked in assessment for over 30 years for international testing organizations. She has designed and delivered courses in assessment literacy and is also the author of several EL exam coursebooks for leading publishers. She is an Associate Tutor (M.A. TESOL/Linguistics) at University College, London. Her research interests are classroom assessment, issues in managing feedback, and intercultural competences.

VOCABULARY CONSULTANT **Cheryl Boyd Zimmerman** is Professor Emeritus at California State University, Fullerton.
She specialized in second-language vocabulary acquisition, an area in which she is widely published. She taught graduate courses on second-language acquisition, culture, vocabulary, and the fundamentals of TESOL, and has been a frequent invited speaker on topics related to vocabulary teaching and learning. She is the author of *Word Knowledge: A Vocabulary Teacher's Handbook* and Series Director of *Inside Reading, Inside Writing*, and *Inside Listening and Speaking*, published by Oxford University Press.

ONLINE INTEGRATION **Chantal Hemmi** holds an Ed.D. TEFL and is a Japan-based teacher trainer and curriculum designer. Since leaving her position as Academic Director of the British Council in Tokyo, she has been teaching at the Center for Language Education and Research at Sophia University in an EAP/CLIL program offered for undergraduates. She delivers lectures and teacher trainings throughout Japan, Indonesia, and Malaysia.

COMMUNICATIVE GRAMMAR CONSULTANT **Nancy Schoenfeld** holds an M.A. in TESOL from Biola University in La Mirada, California, and has been an English language instructor since 2000. She has taught ESL in California and Hawaii and EFL in Thailand and Kuwait. She has also trained teachers in the United States and Indonesia. Her interests include teaching vocabulary, extensive reading, and student motivation. She is currently an English Language Instructor at Kuwait University.

CONTENTS

Welcome to *Q: Skills for Success* Third Edition iv
What is iQ Online? viii
Authors and Consultants x

UNIT 5 Psychology – How do people overcome obstacles? 104
Reading 1: How People Learn to Become Resilient 106
Critical Thinking Strategy: Justifying your opinion of a text 110
Reading Skill: Using referents to understand contrast 113
Reading 2: The Climb of My Life 115
Work with the Video: Shona Regains Her Confidence 120
Vocabulary Skill: Using the dictionary to find the correct meaning 121
Writing Skill: Writing a narrative essay 123
Grammar: Shifts between past and present time frames 126
Unit Assignment: Write a narrative essay 127

UNIT 6 Neurology – Are you a good decision maker? 130
Reading 1: The Lazy Brain 132
Reading Skill: Using a graphic organizer 138
Reading 2: Problem-Solvers: Which One Are You? 139
Critical Thinking Strategy: Classifying Information 144
Work with the Video: Intuition 146
Vocabulary Skill: Phrasal verbs 147
Writing Skill: Stating reasons and giving examples 149
Grammar: Gerunds and infinitives 153
Unit Assignment: Write an analysis essay with reasons and examples 155

UNIT 7 Economics – Can a business earn money while making a difference? 158
Reading 1: FEED Projects: How a Bag Can Feed Children in Many Ways 160
Reading Skill: Using a timeline 165
Reading 2: A New Business Model: Do Well While Doing Good 167
Critical Thinking Strategy: Adding details to support statements 174
Work with the Video: Ecotourism 175
Vocabulary Skill: Collocations with verbs 176
Writing Skill: Writing a cause/effect essay 177
Grammar: Complex sentences 181
Unit Assignment: Write a cause/effect essay 183

UNIT 8 Behavioral Studies – What does it take to be successful? 186
Reading 1: Fast Cars, Big Money 188
Reading Skill: Scanning a text 192
Reading 2: Practice Makes . . . Pain? 193
Critical Thinking Strategy: Identifying problems and solutions 197
Work with the Video: Sports Scholarships in the USA 199
Vocabulary Skill: Collocations with adjectives + prepositions 200
Writing Skill: Writing an argumentative essay 202
Grammar: Sentence fragments 206
Unit Assignment: Write an argumentative essay 207

Vocabulary List and CEFR Correlation 211

Psychology

CRITICAL THINKING justifying your opinion of a text
READING using referents to understand contrast
VOCABULARY using the dictionary to find the correct meaning
WRITING writing a narrative essay
GRAMMAR shifts between past and present time frames

 **UNIT QUESTION**

How do people overcome obstacles?

A. Discuss these questions with your classmates.

1. What is an obstacle? Describe different types of obstacles that can occur.

2. Do you know someone who overcame an obstacle? What kind of obstacle was it?

3. Look at the photo. What kinds of challenges does the man have? What qualities or characteristics do you think might help him?

B. Listen to *The Q Classroom* online. Then answer these questions.

1. Sophy thinks that it's important to have someone to support you. Why do you think that's important for overcoming obstacles or challenges in your life? Give examples of people who could help someone overcome obstacles.

2. Felix thinks that there are characteristics that a person has that will help him or her overcome challenges. Do you agree with that? What qualities do you think will help you face difficulties in your life?

iQ PRACTICE Go to the online discussion board to discuss the Unit Question with your classmates. *Practice > Unit 5 > Activity 1*

UNIT OBJECTIVE

Read the article and book excerpt and gather information and ideas to write a narrative essay about an obstacle that you've faced.

READING

READING 1

How People Learn to Become Resilient

OBJECTIVE ▶

You are going to read an article from the *New Yorker* about resilience. *Resilience* means being strong enough to recover quickly from damage, an illness, a shock, or change. The article discusses research into how some people are resilient. Use the article to gather information and ideas for your Unit Assignment.

PREVIEW THE READING

A. PREVIEW Read the title and first paragraph. How would you describe the boy in the article? Check (✓) your answers.

☐ He has a good home life.

☐ He's a happy person.

☐ He's unlucky.

☐ He feels sorry for himself.

☐ He makes the most of his situation.

B. QUICK WRITE Think about an obstacle or challenge that you've overcome. Write for 5–10 minutes in response. Remember to use this section for your Unit Assignment.

C. VOCABULARY Check (✓) the words you know. Then work with a partner to locate each word in the reading. Use clues to help define the words you don't know. Check your definitions in the dictionary.

element *(n.)* OPAL	poverty *(n.)* OPAL	trait *(n.)*
emerge *(v.)* OPAL	predict *(v.)* OPAL	traumatic *(adj.)*
enable *(v.)* OPAL	set apart *(v. phr.)*	
perceive *(v.)* OPAL	threat *(n.)* OPAL	

Oxford 3000™ words   OPAL Oxford Phrasal Academic Lexicon

iQ PRACTICE Go online to listen and practice your pronunciation.
Practice > Unit 5 > Activity 2

WORK WITH THE READING

 A. INVESTIGATE Read the article and gather information about how people overcome obstacles.

How People Learn to Become Resilient

By Maria Konnikova

1   Norman Garmezy, a psychologist at the University of Minnesota, met thousands of children in his four decades of research. But one boy in particular stuck with him. He was nine years old, with an ill mother and an absent father. Each day, he would arrive at school with the exact same sandwich: two slices of bread with nothing in between. At home, there was no other food available and no one to make any. Even so, Garmezy would later recall, the boy wanted to make sure that "no one would feel pity for him." Each day, without fail, he would walk in with a smile on his face and a "bread sandwich" tucked into his bag.

2   The boy with the bread sandwich was part of a special group of children. Garmezy identified this group of kids as succeeding, even excelling, despite incredibly difficult circumstances. These were the children who exhibited a **trait** Garmezy would later identify as "resilience."

3   Resilience presents a challenge for psychologists. Finding out if you have it or not largely depends on the way your life unfolds. If you are lucky enough to never experience any sort of adversity, we won't know how resilient you are. It's only when you're faced with obstacles, stress, and other environmental **threats** that resilience, or the lack of it, **emerges**: do you fall apart or do you rise above it?

4   Environmental threats can come in various ways. Some are continuous, such as **poverty** and challenging home conditions. Other threats are acute: experiencing or witnessing a **traumatic** violent encounter, for example, or being in an accident. What matters is the intensity and the duration of the stressful event.

5   Garmezy's work looked at protective factors: the **elements** of an individual's background or personality that could **enable** success despite the challenges the person faced. His research

identified elements that fell into two groups: individual psychological factors and external environmental factors.

6   In 1989, a psychologist named Emmy Werner published the results of a 32-year project. She had followed a group of 698 children in Kauai, Hawaii, from before birth through their third decade of life. Along the way, she'd monitored them for any exposure to stress: poverty, problems in the family, and so on. Two-thirds of the children came from backgrounds that were essentially stable, successful, and happy; the other third qualified as "at risk." Like Garmezy, she soon discovered that not all of the at-risk children reacted to stress in the same way. Two-thirds of them "developed serious learning or behavior problems by the age of ten," or had other more serious mental health and behavior problems as they became older. But the remaining third developed into "competent, confident, and caring young adults." They had attained academic, domestic, and social success—and they were always ready to take advantage of new opportunities that arose.

7   What was it that **set** the resilient children **apart**? She found that several elements **predicted** resilience. Some elements had to do with luck: a resilient child might have a strong bond with a supportive caregiver, parent, teacher, or other mentor-like figure. But another, quite large set of elements was psychological and had to do with how the children responded to the environment. From a young age, resilient children tended to "meet the world on their own terms." They were autonomous and independent, would seek out new experiences, and had a "positive social orientation." Werner wrote, "Though not especially gifted, these children used whatever skills they had effectively." Perhaps most importantly, the resilient children believed that they, and not their circumstances, affected their achievements. The resilient children saw themselves as being able to make good decisions about their obstacles to improve their future.

8   George Bonanno is a clinical psychologist at Columbia University's Teachers College and has been studying resilience for nearly 25 years. Garmezy, Werner, and others have shown that some people are far better than others at dealing with adversity. Bonanno has been trying to figure out where that variation might come from. One of the central elements of resilience, Bonanno has found, is perception: Do you **perceive** an event as traumatic or as an opportunity to learn and grow? "Events are not traumatic until we experience them as traumatic," Bonanno told me. Take something as terrible as the surprising death of a close friend: you might be sad, but if you can find a way to see that event as filled with meaning—perhaps it leads to greater awareness of a certain disease or to closer ties with the community—then it may not be seen as a trauma. The good news is that positive interpretation can be taught. "We can make ourselves more or less vulnerable by how we think about things," Bonanno said.

B. VOCABULARY Here are some words from Reading 1. Read the sentences. Then match each bold word with its definition below.

___ 1. The teacher **predicted** that the students would do well on the achievement test if they continued to do all of their assignments.

___ 2. There are many **elements** involved in being a successful student, such as determination and hard work.

___ 3. Even though he grew up in **poverty**, he was able to succeed in life by working hard and focusing on his education.

___ 4. Many people go through **traumatic** events as children, such as the death of a parent.

___ 5. When someone has an experience in a different country, it **sets** them **apart** from others who never left their homeland.

___ 6. Receiving a seeing-eye dog **enabled** the blind woman to travel to places on her own.

___ 7. Olivia **emerged** as a very competent and confident young woman even though she was very shy as a child.

___ 8. The **threat** of losing his job was a constant fear in his life after he received a poor evaluation from his boss.

___ 9. Some people **perceive** a challenge as stressful, while others see it as a new opportunity for personal growth.

___ 10. One **trait** that resilient people share is that they feel that they are in control of their lives.

a. *(n.)* a quality or part of someone's character

b. *(v.)* to appear or come from somewhere unexpectedly

c. *(n.)* the state of having very little money or of being poor

d. *(n.)* an important part of something

e. *(v.)* to see or think of something in a particular way

f. *(v.)* to make someone able to do something

g. *(v.)* to say that something will happen

h. *(n.)* something that indicates future danger

i. *(v. phr.)* to make something different from or better than others

j. *(adj.)* causing someone to feel great unhappiness or shock

iQ PRACTICE Go online for more practice with the vocabulary.
Practice > Unit 5 > Activity 3

CRITICAL THINKING STRATEGY

Justifying your opinion of a text

As readers, we often form opinions about the ideas or statements made in an article. Do we agree with a statement? Does it seem true based on our experience? Good writers support their statements with evidence, for example, from research or from facts and statistics. Before you decide if you agree or disagree with an idea in a text, think about the evidence the writer has provided. Does the evidence **justify your opinion**? Can you give reasons and examples for or against the statements made in the text? You can use knowledge and personal experience to help form your opinion and make it stronger with information from your own research, for example, from reading more articles on the same topic. You can ask:

- *Is the statement supported by evidence?* (Find the evidence in the text.)
- *What kind of evidence is it?* (e.g., research, facts, statistics)
- *The text quotes a study: Was it a good study?* (e.g., involved lots of people, collected lots of data)
- *Do other studies support the idea?* (Do online research.)

Use this information to decide if you agree with the ideas in a text and to justify your opinion in discussions or essays on the topic.

iQ PRACTICE Go online to watch the Critical Thinking Video and check your comprehension. *Practice › Unit 5 › Activity 4*

C. IDENTIFY Read the ideas below. Find the evidence in the text for each idea. Then decide if you agree or disagree.

Idea in text	Agree/Disagree?	Ways to justify opinion
1. Only certain people going through difficult challenges have a quality called *resilience*.	agree	good evidence in text: very long study (32 years) with lots of people (698) check online for more studies
2. There are many factors that predict a person's resilience.		
3. The way people perceive events affects their resilience.		
4. Positive perceptions can be taught.		

D. EXTEND Work with a partner. How can you justify your opinion of the statements? Use the information in the chart and your own ideas. Think of as many ways as you can.

E. CATEGORIZE Read the statements. Write *T* (true) or *F* (false). Then correct each false statement to make it true according to the article.

____ 1. The boy who Norman Garmezy describes came to school every day with a cheese sandwich and a smile on his face.

____ 2. When you are resilient, you rise above a situation that is stressful.

____ 3. An example of a continuous threat, according to Garmezy, is being in an accident.

____ 4. Emmy Werner found in her study of 698 children that they all reacted to stress in the same way.

____ 5. One-third of the children Werner studied became successful adults.

____ 6. According to Werner, the resilient children believed that their life circumstances affected how successful they would be.

____ 7. George Bonanno believes that the key to resilience is how you perceive an event.

F. IDENTIFY Complete the statements with information from the reading. Then write the paragraph number where the answer is found.

1. Some people belong to a group that succeeds even though they live in _____. Paragraph ____

2. Environmental threats can be either continuous or _____. Paragraph ____

3. Emmy Werner studied children for more than _____ years. Paragraph ____

4. Two-thirds of the children she studied came from _____ homes. Paragraph ____

5. Of the "at risk" children that Werner studied, two-thirds of these children had _____ as they became older. Paragraph ____

6. Werner found that the resilient children had an element of luck, which she described as a bond with _____. Paragraph ____

7. Werner described these resilient children as _____. Paragraph ____

8. Bonanno also feels that positive interpretation of events is something that we can _____. Paragraph ____

G. **IDENTIFY** Read the statements. Identify which researcher discovered this information. Write the letter of the researcher. There may be more than one answer.

G (Norman Garmezy)   W (Emmy Werner)   B (George Bonanno)

___ 1. How long and how intense a threat is to someone will affect how resilient they are.

___ 2. A stressful event will only be traumatic if we perceive it that way.

___ 3. There are always some people who respond in a positive way to traumatic events.

___ 4. Two-thirds of the children who grew up in very bad situations developed serious behavior problems.

___ 5. Resilient people take control of their obstacles by making good decisions, rather than letting their circumstances control them.

___ 6. There are certain factors in one's personality or environment that can help them to deal with stress.

H. **EXPAND** Look back at your Quick Write on page 106. How do you think you overcame the obstacle? Was it because someone helped you? Or was it the way you perceived the challenge that helped you to deal with it. Or is it a characteristic in your personality that helped you? Add any new ideas or information you learned from the reading.

iQ PRACTICE Go online for additional reading and comprehension.
Practice > Unit 5 > Activity 5

WRITE WHAT YOU THINK

A. DISCUSS Discuss the questions in a group. Think about the Unit Question, "How do people overcome obstacles?"

1. Do you see yourself as resilient? Are there certain factors that can explain how resilient you are? Do you think that your resilience depends on how serious the challenge is?

2. Look back at the photo on page 108. How do you think the man was able to deal with losing his home? What type of person do you think does the best in dealing with an obstacle like this?

3. Some people see a glass as half full, while others see it as half empty. What does this mean about the perception of the water in the glass? Do you perceive difficulties in a positive way?

B. CREATE Choose one of the questions from Activity A and write a paragraph in response. Look back at your Quick Write on page 106 as you think about what you learned.

READING SKILL Using referents to understand contrast

A **referent** is a word or group of words that refers to a noun that was mentioned previously. Understanding referents will help you become a better reader. In Reading 1, the writer is focusing on what makes one group of people more resilient than others. The writer uses certain words and phrases to refer to this particular group and to the factors leading to resilience throughout the reading.

Words like *this* and *these* refer back to the noun being focused on.

> The boy with the bread sandwich was part of a special group of children. These children stood out from others in similar situations. Garmezy identified this group of kids as succeeding . . .

Words like *some* and *other* show differences among groups of things but still refer back to the noun being focused on.

> Environmental threats can come in various ways. Some are continuous . . . Other threats are acute . . .

> She found that several elements predicted resilience. Some elements had to do with luck . . . But another, quite large set of elements was psychological.

A. IDENTIFY Read the sentences and look at the words in bold. Circle the noun that they refer to.

1. Many children face obstacles growing up, but **some** children seem to deal with **these** problems better than **others**.

2. The resilient children displayed a certain kind of personality. **These** children felt they were in control of their life circumstances. Other children felt that their circumstance would never improve.

3. The researchers discovered that there are several elements that help someone be resilient. **Some** of the elements are environmental. **Others** are psychological.

4. Resilient people tend to look at adversity differently. **These** people see obstacles as opportunities for growth. Others tend to feel overwhelmed by life's challenges.

5. Resilience is something that can be taught. **This** quality can develop when we perceive problems differently.

ACADEMIC LANGUAGE

The phrase *tend to* is often used in academic writing. It is more appropriate in an academic context than *usually*.

OPAL
Oxford Phrasal Academic Lexicon

B. RECOGNIZE Read the paragraph about resilient people. Underline the words and phrases that refer to resilient people. Circle the words and phrases that refer to other types of people.

Some people see the glass as half full, and others see it as half empty. The first group has a trait we call resilience. When adversity strikes, this group of people tends to look at the problem in a positive light. For example, say you lose your job because of cutbacks at your company. A resilient person will look at this not as an obstacle to overcome, but as a new opportunity. Maybe this person has never had the time to look at other employment opportunities. Maybe this person will decide to go back to school to change careers. The difference between resilient people and others is that they perceive the challenges differently. Other people might be depressed and stressed over losing their job, but resilient people, though they might be stressed at first, have the ability to bounce back and use the challenge as a way to see and do things differently.

iQ PRACTICE Go online for more practice with using referents to understand contrast. *Practice > Unit 5 > Activity 6*

READING 2

The Climb of My Life

OBJECTIVE ▶ You are going to read an excerpt from a book called *The Climb of My Life: Scaling Mountains with a Borrowed Heart* by Kelly Perkins. It's about a woman who climbs a mountain ten months after having a heart transplant. A transplant is a type of surgery in which an organ, for example, a heart, liver, or kidney, is replaced. Use the reading to gather information and ideas for your Unit Assignment.

PREVIEW THE READING

A. PREVIEW Read the title and first two paragraphs. Why do you think Kelly Perkins felt that she needed to climb a mountain? Check (✓) your answer.

☐ She wanted to improve her health.

☐ She wanted to improve how she felt about herself.

☐ She likes the excitement of mountain climbing.

B. QUICK WRITE Think about a time when you had a challenge in life, perhaps a physical challenge like an illness. What did you do to help you overcome this challenge? Write for 5–10 minutes in response. Be sure to use this section for your Unit Assignment.

C. VOCABULARY Check (✓) the words you know. Use a dictionary to define any new or unknown words. Then discuss how the words will relate to the unit with a partner.

bravely *(adv.)*	distinctive *(adj.)* OPAL	role *(n.)* OPAL
conquer *(v.)*	earn *(v.)*	significant *(adj.)* OPAL
determined *(adj.)*	goal *(n.)* OPAL	ultimate *(adj.)* OPAL

Oxford 3000™ words OPAL Oxford Phrasal Academic Lexicon

iQ PRACTICE Go online to listen and practice your pronunciation.
Practice › Unit 5 › Activity 7

WORK WITH THE READING

 A. INVESTIGATE Read the excerpt and gather information about why people take risks.

THE CLIMB OF MY LIFE

1 At the age of 30, Kelly Perkins developed a disease of the heart, and after three years of treatment, she received a heart transplant. Ten months later, she climbed to the top of Half Dome Mountain in Yosemite National Park in the United States and became the first heart transplant patient to do so.

2 Like life, mountains can be seen as a series of difficulties that you need to overcome. To me, a mountain is the **ultimate** challenge, with body, spirit, and mind all having to work together. Being sick is a challenge, too. Both challenges involve **bravely** facing the unknown, and to **conquer** either requires well-defined **goals** and discipline. Of the two, of course, I'd rather the mountain be my physical challenge than physical challenges be my "mountain."

3 Mountains began to consume my thoughts. Secretly, I wanted to do something **significant** to help change the image that friends and family had developed of me. I had been cast in the **role** of patient. In spite of being very good in that role, I hated being a patient and desperately wanted to change my image. I wanted bruises to be **earned** from sports-related activities, not from needle pricks and aspirin-thinned blood. At this stage, my self-image was as important to my well-being as anything else. If, I figured, I could rebuild my strength and regain at least some of my former athleticism, an improved image would naturally follow.

4 I set a goal—to hike the 4,100-foot ascent of Half Dome in Yosemite. I was drawn to this destination by its beauty, a beauty not because it was perfect, but because it was imperfect. Half Dome's shape is unforgettably **distinctive** because it's broken. If it were whole, it would lose its uniqueness. The spirit-building message wasn't lost on me. Just because I wasn't perfect didn't mean I couldn't stand as tall and mighty as anyone else.

116   UNIT 5   How do people overcome obstacles?

5   In August of 1996, just ten months after my heart replacement, my husband Craig and I began to hike the trail leading to Half Dome. The trail began with a mild incline, which we eagerly took at a brisk pace. I was winded at first, but as soon as my heart caught up with me, I felt energized. I tried to go as fast as the other hikers, but found it difficult to keep up. The canyon had many steep slopes and deep stone stairs, allowing in very little sunlight, which kept temperatures cool and the rocks slippery.

6   Though the climb's final half-mile isn't technically difficult, the granite dome, angled at 45 degrees, can be extremely intimidating, especially for those afraid of heights. A stairway is used to climb the last 500 feet to the summit. There was a handrail made out of steel cables, connected to stairs made of thin wooden planks. Thrown along the stairs were weathered work gloves, available to help protect the climbers' hands from the "death grip" commonly used during descent. Craig, observing the daunting task ahead, gently asked, "Are you sure you want to continue?"

Determined to reap[1] the reward for all my effort, I replied, "Absolutely, we have to go on." Step for step, Craig stayed directly behind me, providing a welcome sense of security. When I finally reached the top, I was overcome with joy. Ten months after my transplant, I had reached the top of Half Dome! My new heart had not failed me.

7   Craig and I made our way over to the edge. Pausing to peer into the valley below, we stood in silence, amazed at how far we had come. As if the moment itself was not enough, Craig surprised me with a gold charm[2] in the shape of Half Dome. He said, "This is the first mountain to add to the bracelet I gave you." As I held the handcrafted ornament in my hand, I was amazed at its likeness. It was smooth on the back, resembling the perfectly bell-shaped dome, the front being chiseled, replicating its famous broken granite face. Craig took a moment to express how proud he was of me, saying, "When you were really sick and I had to help you up the stairs at night, I always looked at the famous Ansel Adams photo of Half Dome hung on the stairway wall and wondered if we'd ever make another climb." We had done it; we were here at the top of the mountain—a long way from those nights of not knowing what the future would bring.

[1] **reap:** to receive a benefit due to one's efforts
[2] **charm:** a small piece of jewelry often worn on bracelets

VOCABULARY SKILL REVIEW

In Unit 3, you learned that synonyms are words that have similar meanings. Can you think of any synonyms for the vocabulary words in Activity B?

B. VOCABULARY Complete each sentence with the vocabulary from Reading 2.

bravely *(adv.)*	distinctive *(adj.)*	role *(n.)*
conquer *(v.)*	earn *(v.)*	significant *(adj.)*
determined *(adj.)*	goal *(n.)*	ultimate *(adj.)*

1. My _____ for this year is to train until I am ready to run the city marathon.

2. My husband took a class that helped him _____ his fear of flying. Now he can ride in airplanes without feeling so nervous.

3. We were very tired, but we didn't give up. We were _____ to get to the top of the mountain.

4. The firefighters _____ entered the burning school to rescue the children.

5. When our parents were away, my oldest brother took on the _____ of the family guardian.

6. I always recognize Dina on the phone because she has a very _____ voice. She doesn't sound like any of my other friends.

7. When we were children, we had to do work around the house in order to _____ rewards like toys or candy.

8. Rock climbing is the _____ activity for people who want a fun, exciting challenge.

9. Volunteering in South America was one of the most _____ experiences of my life. It inspired me to pursue a career in public service.

iQ PRACTICE Go online for more practice with the vocabulary.
Practice > Unit 5 > Activity 8

C. IDENTIFY Read the sentences. Then number them in the order that the events happened.

____ 1. Perkins decided to climb Half Dome Mountain in Yosemite.

____ 2. Ten months after her heart replacement, Perkins began to climb Half Dome.

____ 3. Perkins decided that she wanted to climb a mountain to change her image.

____ 4. Kelly Perkins became very sick and received a heart transplant.

____ 5. Craig was proud of his wife's accomplishment.

____ 6. Perkins reached the top of Half Dome with a new heart.

D. INTERPRET Read the summary statements. Then write the number of the paragraph that each statement summarizes.

____ 1. I'd prefer to be challenged by mountain climbing and not illness.

____ 2. I hoped to stand tall, but imperfect, like the mountain I chose to climb.

____ 3. The last part of the mountain is so steep that there are stairs to help people climb to the top, and I was going to be one of those people.

____ 4. I missed extreme physical activity and needed to prove to my family and friends, and more importantly, to myself, that I could still do it.

E. RESTATE Complete each statement with information from Reading 2. Then write the paragraph number where the answer is found.

1. Kelly Perkins chose a mountain to climb that is _____ feet high. Paragraph: ____

2. One reason she chose this mountain is because, like her, it is _____. Paragraph: ____

3. Perkins began her climb of Half Dome with her husband in August of _____. Paragraph: ____

4. The last half-mile of the climb is hard if you're afraid of heights because it's angled at _____ degrees. Paragraph: ____

5. There is a rough stairway to help climbers for the last _____ feet. Paragraph: ____

6. Perkins's husband Craig said it was the first mountain to add to a(n) _____ that he had given her. Paragraph: ____

F. CATEGORIZE Read the statements. Write *T* (true) or *F* (false) and the paragraph number where the answer is found. Then correct each false statement to make it true according to the article.

____ 1. Kelly Perkins didn't want her husband to climb directly behind her. Paragraph: ____

____ 2. Craig was confident before this climb that they would be climbing mountains again. Paragraph: ____

____ 3. Perkins had trouble when she began the climb up Half Dome Mountain. Paragraph: ____

____ 4. Perkins used to be very athletic before she got sick. Paragraph: ____

____ 5. The gloves on the stairs of Half Dome are to help people going up the mountain. Paragraph: ____

G. DISCUSS Discuss the questions in a group. Look back at your Quick Write on page 115 as you think about what you learned.

1. In paragraph 2, Kelly Perkins talks about challenges—climbing mountains and being sick—and says, "Of the two, of course, I'd rather the mountain be my physical challenge than physical challenges be my 'mountain.'"
What does this mean for Perkins?

2. Perkins climbed mountains before and after her heart transplant. Do you think the reasons for climbing mountains were different before and after her transplant? Why or why not?

WORK WITH THE VIDEO

VIDEO VOCABULARY

deal with (v. phr.) to act in a suitable way in order to solve a problem, complete a task, etc.; to handle something

control of (n. phr.) power over something; the ability to organize, direct, or guide somebody or something

panic (v.) to have a sudden feeling of fear that makes you act without thinking carefully

keep up with (v. phr.) to continue to do something to be on the same level as others

look forward to (v. phr.) to wait with pleasure for something to happen (because you expect to enjoy it)

A. PREVIEW Did you ever have a bad experience doing something that made you fearful of doing it again?

iQ RESOURCES Go online to watch the video about a young girl named Shona, who is learning to ride a horse again after getting hurt. *Resources > Video > Unit 5 > Unit Video*

B. CATEGORIZE Watch the video two or three times. Then take notes in the first part of the chart.

	How Shona felt when she first arrived at the riding school	How she overcame her fear of riding
Notes from the video		
My ideas		

C. EXTEND What do you think was the biggest factor in helping Shona to overcome her fear? Write your ideas in the chart above.

WRITE WHAT YOU THINK

SYNTHESIZE Think about Reading 1, Reading 2, and the unit video as you discuss these questions. Then choose one question and write a paragraph in response.

1. Do you think that people who had very bad childhoods could forget about their past? In other words, do you think they need to move past their previous difficulties and focus on the present?

2. Do you think people can change the way they perceive challenges or obstacles? Are there certain situations or times in people's lives that we perceive as traumatic? Is there another way to look at these experiences?

VOCABULARY SKILL Using the dictionary to find the correct meaning

Words often have more than one meaning. When dictionaries include more than one meaning, the different definitions are usually numbered. When you are using a dictionary to find the **correct meaning** for a word, it is important to read the entire sentence and consider the context.

Look at the example and the dictionary definitions that follow it. Definition 4 is correct.

> Mountains began to **consume** my thoughts.

> **con·sume** /kən'sum/ *verb* [T] *(formal)* **1** to use something such as fuel, energy, or time: *25 percent of the world's population consumes 80 percent of the planet's resources.* **2** to eat or drink something: *to consume calories* **3** (used about fire) to destroy something **4** (used about an emotion) to affect someone very strongly: *She was consumed by grief when her son was killed.*

All dictionary entries adapted from the *Oxford American Dictionary for learners of English* © Oxford University Press 2011.

A. Read these sentences from the readings. Look up the underlined words in your dictionary and write the correct definition based on the context. Then compare your answers with a partner.

1. Do you <u>fall apart</u> or <u>rise</u> above it?

   fall apart: _____

   rise above: _____

2. From a young age, resilient children tended to <u>meet</u> the world on their own terms.

   meet: _____

3. I had been cast in the role of patient.

   role: _____

4. I wanted bruises to be earned from sports-related activities, not from needle pricks and aspirin-thinned blood.

   earned: _____

5. It was smooth on the back, resembling the perfectly bell-shaped dome, the front being chiseled, replicating its famous broken granite face.

   face: _____

B. Choose three words from Activity A. Write a sentence using each word.

1. _____
   _____

2. _____
   _____

3. _____
   _____

iQ PRACTICE Go online for more practice with using the dictionary to find the correct meaning. *Practice › Unit 5 › Activity 9*

WRITING

OBJECTIVE ▶ At the end of this unit, you will write a narrative essay about an obstacle that you have faced. This essay will include specific information from the readings, the unit video, and your own ideas.

WRITING SKILL Writing a narrative essay

A **narrative essay** tells the story of a personal experience or event. The introductory paragraph of a narrative essay gives necessary background information and then explains why this is an important or memorable story for the writer. This main idea is included in the thesis statement.

A narrative essay also contains the other important parts of an essay, including two to three body paragraphs and a concluding paragraph. The body paragraphs describe the events and include details, such as facts, examples, or explanations, to support the thesis statement or main idea of the essay. The concluding paragraph restates the main idea and summarizes why this story is an important one for the writer.

A. WRITING MODEL Read the model narrative essay.

When I graduated from college, I took a two-week vacation to the West Coast before starting my job as a teacher in New York City. My friend Sophia and I planned to drive up the coast from Los Angeles to San Francisco. It was the third day of the trip and our first day of rain. As I was driving up Route 1, the rain became heavier. Suddenly, a truck approached on the opposite side of the road. The truck was dangerously close to our car as we went around a sharp curve. And that's the last thing I remember. That day would change my life forever.

When I woke up, I was in a hospital in California. My parents were there, looking very concerned. I was a bit disoriented, and my mother explained that there had been a terrible accident. Sophia was fine and had gone home to her family. And I was going to be fine, though not completely. My right leg had been so damaged in the accident that they had to amputate it. I had lost my leg. I was completely devastated.

Over the next few months, I focused mainly on regaining my health. There were certainly ups and downs, but when I got depressed, my mom helped me see that I was lucky to be alive. As I got stronger, I had to learn to deal with having only one leg. When my injury had healed enough, I had to learn to walk again—with only one leg. It was very painful in the beginning. I tried not to think about how the rest of my life was going to unfold. I just focused on getting stronger and on learning to walk on my new leg, an artificial one.

About six months after my accident, I was ready to begin my new life. I had gotten fairly good at walking on my prosthetic leg, and I found out about a group that helped people deal with injuries like mine, Achilles International. They worked out together in Central Park every week. Since I had been a runner on the track team in college, it seemed like a good fit for me. Every month they had short races in Central Park. I thought, "What have I got to lose?" I finished my race, but more importantly, I had accomplished something that a few months before I had thought would be impossible. Also, I met people who I could help, people who had injuries or physical challenges far worse than mine. It helped me see that my injury, though very serious, was not really going to change my life. I would still be able to continue with my dreams and my life goals. It was just "a bump in the road of life" that I had to come to terms with.

It's now a year later, and I'm finally teaching in the school I had planned to be in a year ago. I have gotten accustomed to wearing my new leg and have even gotten another one, specifically for running. I'm still involved with Achilles International and plan to run the marathon this fall. I acknowledge that my life has changed, but I am still the same person inside.

B. EVALUATE Reread the narrative essay in Activity A. Then answer the questions.

1. Where does the writer give background information? Put a check mark (✓) next to it.

2. Which sentence in the introductory paragraph includes the main idea (thesis statement) of the narrative? Write it below.

_____

_____

3. How many body paragraphs does the writer include? Mark the body paragraph(s) with brackets. ([ ])

4. What details does the writer include to help show the passage of time. Underline them.

5. Which sentence in the concluding paragraph explains why this story is important to the writer? Write it below.

_____

_____

C. **WRITING MODEL** Read the model narrative essay. Then answer the questions below.

> The storm began quickly and wildly. I was sitting in my living room watching the ocean as the waves grew in size and strength. Many people told me I was foolish to stay in my house and not seek shelter away from the beach. But this was my home. I had always stayed put during previous hurricanes, and this was no exception. _____
> _____
>
> The ferocious winds died down almost as quickly as they had started. As I inspected my house, I realized the basement contained two feet of water. Fortunately, I had removed anything valuable before the storm. Then I noticed the flood of water running down the street. The street was no more, replaced by a river running through the neighborhood. As I was surveying the area, I heard shouts from down the street. I walked out to the garage and grabbed my kayak. This would provide my transportation for the next few hours.
>
> I paddled down the street to where the shouts were coming from. One of my neighbors had also stayed in his house, but the water had poured into the second floor. He and his family, including two small children, were left with only the attic to stay in. I tied a rope to each of the children and placed them into the kayak. I paddled them to the end of the street where the water subsided and pavement was visible. We finally reached an undamaged home, and I lifted the children to safety. Then I returned to help their parents.
>
> Though the flooding went on through the night, the damage had been done in minutes. Some people thought I should not have stayed in the house, but saving my neighbor and his family was proof enough for me that I had made the right decision.

1. Which sentence is the best thesis statement for the essay? Discuss your choice with a partner. Write the thesis statement in the introductory paragraph.

    a. Hurricanes are very exciting, so I wanted to stay and see as much as I could.

    b. I felt confident that nothing was going to happen to my house, so I made my decision to stay and watch it.

    c. I knew it could be dangerous, but I thought maybe I could help others who might be in need.

2. Underline any background information in the introductory paragraph.

3. Look at the concluding paragraph. Underline the words that restate the main idea and summarize why this story is important to the writer.

iQ PRACTICE Go online for more practice with writing a narrative essay.
Practice › Unit 5 › Activity 10

GRAMMAR Shifts between past and present time frames

A written essay or passage begins with a specific **time frame**, such as past, present, or future. Sometimes writers use one time frame for the entire passage, but often they shift or change time frames. Writers shift time frames according to what they are describing.

Writers often use the **simple past** to begin a story, or set the scene.

> simple past
> A few months after the Half Dome climb, I **decided** to climb Mt. Whitney in California.

Writers use the **past perfect** to describe things that happened before the events in the story. Use *had* + **past participle** to form the past perfect.

> simple past
> Secretly, I **wanted** to do something significant to help change the image that
> past perfect
> friends and family **had developed** of me.

Writers use the **simple present** to describe things or give certain facts or information.

> simple present   simple present
> Half Dome's shape **is** unforgettably distinctive because it**'s** broken.

iQ RESOURCES Go online to watch the Grammar Skill Video.
Resources › Video › Unit 5 › Grammar Skill Video

A. IDENTIFY Look back at the model narrative essay on page 123. Draw a box around the simple past verbs and past perfect verbs. Circle the simple present verbs. Then compare your answers with a partner.

B. EXTEND Read the short passages. Write *present* if the passage uses only a present time frame. Write *past* if the passage uses only a past time frame. Write *present/past* or *past/present* if the passage changes time frames.

past/present   1. Three years ago, I went hiking in the White Mountains in New Hampshire. New Hampshire is a beautiful place to hike with lots of lakes and mountains.

_____   2. The storm last week caused a lot of damage, and many people could not get to work or school. Now the roads are clear, and businesses and schools are open again.

126 UNIT 5 How do people overcome obstacles?

_____ 3. Florence, Italy, is a wonderful place to spend a vacation. There are lots of interesting things to do and see.

_____ 4. Last year, Amy decided to try rock climbing. It was something she had always wanted to try.

_____ 5. Mountain climbing is exciting, but it can be dangerous. Last year, there were hundreds of accidents.

C. COMPOSE Complete each sentence using a different time frame.

1. I used to drive to work, but now *I ride my bike* _____.

2. I used to drink soda every day. Now _____.

3. When I was younger, I didn't speak English very well. Now _____
   _____.

4. Many things are different in my country now. For example, in the
   past, _____.

5. I used to eat every meal in a restaurant. I'm trying to save money,
   so now _____.

6. I used to watch TV all weekend, but now _____.

iQ PRACTICE Go online for more practice with shifts between past and present time frames. *Practice › Unit 5 › Activities 11–12*

UNIT ASSIGNMENT   Write a narrative essay

OBJECTIVE ▶

In this assignment, you are going to write a narrative essay about an obstacle that you have faced. Think about how you were able to overcome the obstacle. As you prepare your essay, think about the Unit Question, "How do people overcome obstacles?" Use information from Reading 1, Reading 2, the unit video, and your work in this unit to support your essay. Refer to the Self-Assessment checklist on page 128.

iQ PRACTICE Go online to the Writing Tutor to read a model narrative essay. *Practice › Unit 5 › Activity 13*

PLAN AND WRITE

A. BRAINSTORM Think of and write some obstacles or challenges that you've faced. They can be small or big. Write as many as you can.

B. PLAN Follow these steps to plan your essay.

1. Look at the obstacles you wrote down in Activity A. Choose one of the obstacles to write about for your essay.

2. Write your thesis statement.

iQ RESOURCES Go online to download and complete the outline for your narrative essay. *Resources > Writing Tools > Unit 5 > Outline*

C. WRITE Use your planning notes to write your essay.

1. Write your narrative essay describing an obstacle that you have faced.

2. Look at the Self-Assessment checklist below to guide your writing.

iQ PRACTICE Go online to the Writing Tutor to write your assignment. *Practice > Unit 5 > Activity 14*

REVISE AND EDIT

iQ RESOURCES Go online to download the peer review worksheet. *Resources > Writing Tools > Unit 5 > Peer Review Worksheet*

A. PEER REVIEW Read your partner's essay. Then use the peer review worksheet. Discuss the review with your partner.

B. REWRITE Based on your partner's review, revise and rewrite your essay.

C. EDIT Complete the Self-Assessment checklist as you prepare to write the final draft of your essay. Be prepared to hand in your work or discuss it in class.

SELF-ASSESSMENT	Yes	No
Does the essay begin with an introductory paragraph that describes the obstacle and any important background information?	☐	☐
Does the essay include two body paragraphs that describe the events and provide details?	☐	☐
Does the essay contain a concluding paragraph that restates your obstacle and how you overcame it, and summarizes why the story is important to you?	☐	☐
Does the essay shift between present and past correctly?	☐	☐
Are words used with the correct meaning?	☐	☐
Does the essay include vocabulary from the unit?	☐	☐
Did you check the essay for punctuation, spelling, and grammar?	☐	☐

D. REFLECT Discuss these questions with a partner or group.

1. What is something new you learned in this unit?
2. Look back at the Unit Question—How do people overcome obstacles? Is your answer different now than when you started the unit? If yes, how? Why?

iQ PRACTICE Go to the online discussion board to discuss the questions.
Practice > Unit 5 > Activity 15

TRACK YOUR SUCCESS

iQ PRACTICE Go online to check the words and phrases you have learned in this unit. *Practice > Unit 5 > Activity 16*

Check (✓) the skills you learned. If you need more work on a skill, refer to the page(s) in parentheses.

CRITICAL THINKING	☐ I can justify my opinion of a text. (p. 110)
READING	☐ I can use referents to understand contrast. (p. 113)
VOCABULARY	☐ I can use the dictionary to find correct meanings. (p. 121)
WRITING	☐ I can write a narrative essay. (p. 123)
GRAMMAR	☐ I can use time shifts correctly in narrative writing. (p. 126)
OBJECTIVE ▶	☐ I can gather information and ideas to write a narrative essay about an obstacle that I've faced.

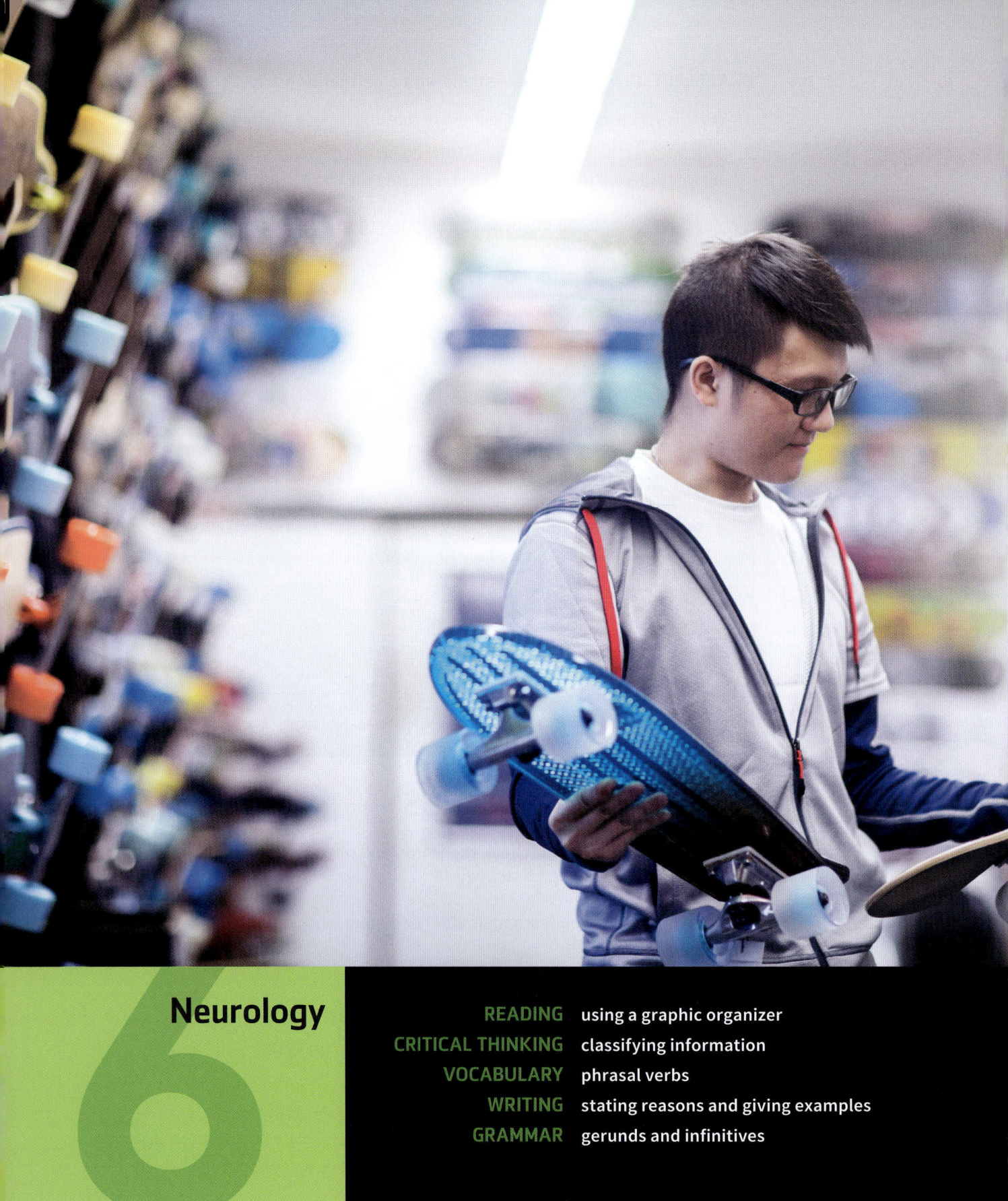

Neurology 6

READING	using a graphic organizer
CRITICAL THINKING	classifying information
VOCABULARY	phrasal verbs
WRITING	stating reasons and giving examples
GRAMMAR	gerunds and infinitives

 **UNIT QUESTION**

Are you a good decision maker?

A. Discuss these questions with your classmates.

1. What is an important decision you made recently in your life? Was it a good decision?
2. Is it easy for you to make big decisions about your life, or is it difficult? Why?
3. Look at the photo. What decision is the man making?

🔊 **B.** Listen to *The Q Classroom* online. Take notes about each person in the chart.

	What decision did he or she make?	Was it a good or bad decision? Why?
Marcus		
Sophy		
Yuna		

iQ PRACTICE Go to the online discussion board to discuss the Unit Question with your classmates. *Practice > Unit 6 > Activity 1*

UNIT OBJECTIVE ▶ Read the articles and gather information and ideas to write an analysis essay about whether you are a good decision maker.

READING

READING 1

The Lazy Brain

OBJECTIVE ▶ You are going to read an article from a science magazine about the effects of lazy thinking. Use the article to gather information and ideas for your Unit Assignment.

PREVIEW THE READING

A. **PREVIEW** Read the title. Read the caption under the first photograph. What do you think the title means by "the lazy brain"?

B. **QUICK WRITE** What was an important decision you made recently? Did you make the right decision? Write for 5–10 minutes in response. Be sure to use this section for your Unit Assignment.

C. **VOCABULARY** Check (✓) the words you know. Then work with a partner to locate each word in the reading. Use clues to help define the words you don't know. Check your definitions in the dictionary.

according to *(prep.)* OPAL	function *(v.)* OPAL	proof *(n.)*
complex *(adj.)* OPAL	make sense *(v. phr.)*	rely on *(v. phr.)*
efficient *(adj.)* OPAL	pace *(n.)*	subject *(n.)* OPAL
experiment *(n.)* OPAL		

🔑 Oxford 3000™ words OPAL Oxford Phrasal Academic Lexicon

iQ PRACTICE Go online to listen and practice your pronunciation.
Practice > Unit 6 > Activity 2

WORK WITH THE READING

 A. INVESTIGATE Read the article and gather information about whether you are a good decision maker.

THE LAZY BRAIN

The lazy brain prefers elevators.

1   If you are a lazy person, don't worry—you might be able to blame your brain! At least, that's what the research suggests.

2   Being lazy doesn't just mean you take the elevator instead of the stairs. It can also mean the way you think and make decisions is "lazy." The problem is that this all happens without our even knowing about it. So, what can we do about it? How can we make our brains less lazy?

3   To understand why the brain wants to be lazy, we must understand how the brain works. The brain is very **complex**, and it actually thinks in two different ways. The first way is the lazy way, and it is a good kind of lazy. It is the thinking we use when we add 1+1. It's the same lazy thinking we use when we drive to school or work. We don't have to think about how to do it—we just do it! **According to** scientists, we have thousands of these lazy thoughts every day.

4   So, why does the brain like lazy decisions? When we do things fast and we don't have to think, we save energy. The brain and body are always trying to save energy. If we save energy, we have more of it, and more energy means we can **function** better in the world. Think about how hard it is to think when we are tired or hungry. We make more mistakes because our brain is too tired.

5   In fact, research has shown that the brain is trying to save energy all the time. In an **experiment** at Simon Fraser University in Canada, scientists wanted to test how good the brain was at saving energy (Selinger et al. 2015). They asked nine **subjects** to walk on a treadmill. The subjects naturally walked at a **pace** that saved the most energy. Then the scientists made it more difficult. They added weight at the knees. As a result, the subjects' original pace was not the most **efficient** anymore. Immediately, they began to walk differently to save as much energy as possible. The brain was saving energy in real time. It happened without them even thinking about it.

6   So, it is good that the brain is lazy because it saves energy. But unfortunately, that's not the whole story. When people **rely on** lazy thinking in situations that require hard thinking, they can run into trouble.

7   For one, lazy thinkers are more likely to believe things without any **proof**. This means that they may accept that something is true even when it isn't. For example, let's say you meet someone new. He tells you, "I'm an honest person," and you assume he is. But in reality, he lies to people, even his friends. Unfortunately, your lazy brain doesn't let you question his honesty. You believe he's a good person because that was the easiest thought.

8   Lazy thinkers are also more likely to make bad decisions. One research study showed that businesspeople with lazy brains have ended up making terrible financial decisions. They didn't think things through; instead, they made quick decisions based on their emotions. Their companies lost money, and some of them lost everything. This is often because people with lazy brains are too confident. Their lazy thinking makes them think they know everything when they really don't.

9   So, how can people fight lazy thinking? Luckily, there is a way. Humans also have another kind of thinking—"hard thinking"—but it takes a lot more energy. Hard thinking is slower. It's the kind of thinking we use when we solve a difficult problem, like 17 x 24. It's the kind of thinking we use when we make more difficult decisions, like when we decide on the career we want or where to live.

10 When we use hard thinking, the body isn't so happy because we are demanding a lot more energy from it. That explains why students get so tired after studying for a test. It explains why long conversations make people want to grab a cup of coffee. They need the caffeine because they feel like they're out of energy. They're not using their lazy brain anymore.

11 The problem is that many people don't use hard thinking enough, and that is what causes problems. So, the advice from scientists is to fight it. In other words, don't just accept everything you hear as true. Question it, and see if it really **makes sense** or not. Don't be too confident about what you know—remember that your first thoughts might be wrong, because they're from your lazy brain. Also, don't forget to take the stairs next time!

References
Selinger, J. et. al. 2015 "Humans Can Continuously Optimize Energetic Cost during Walking," *Current Biology*. September 21, 2015. doi: 10.1016/j.cub.2015.08.016

ACADEMIC LANGUAGE
The corpus shows that *according to* is more common in academic writing than academic speaking.

OPAL
Oxford Phrasal Academic Lexicon

B. VOCABULARY Here are some words from Reading 1. Read the sentences. Then write each bold word next to the correct definition on page 135. You may need to change the form of some of the words.

1. The human brain is able to solve both simple and very **complex** problems.

2. **According to** scientists, the brain works harder when people are sleeping than when they are awake.

3. The brain **functions** similarly to the way a computer works in that it stores information, solves problems, and makes decisions about what to do.

4. In an **experiment** at the University of Southern California, researchers found that studying music at a young age makes children's brains grow faster.

5. The **subjects** in the experiment were children in Los Angeles who received music instruction at school for free.

6. Generally, it is a good idea to walk at a quick **pace** because it makes the heart work harder and burns more calories.

7. Students who work have to find the most **efficient** ways to use their time so that they can have enough time to study and do their homework.

8. People who **rely** too much **on** first impressions can make bad judgments about who someone really is. It takes time to really get to know how another person thinks.

9. Some people believe that dreams are the brain's way of solving problems, but it is very difficult to find **proof** for that because we can't study dreams easily.

10. If the brain likes being lazy, it **makes sense** that people want to get from one place to another in the shortest distance possible.

a. _____ (n.) a scientific test that is done in order to study what happens and to gain new knowledge

b. _____ (n.) the speed at which somebody walks, runs, or moves

c. _____ (v.) to perform a particular job or role

d. _____ (n.) information, documents, etc., that show that something is true

e. _____ (adj.) difficult to understand or deal with

f. _____ (n.) a person being used to study something, especially in an experiment

g. _____ (prep.) as stated or reported by someone or something

h. _____ (v. phr.) to trust or have confidence in somebody or something

i. _____ (v. phr.) to have a meaning that can be understood

j. _____ (adj.) doing something well and with no waste of time, money, or energy

iQ PRACTICE Go online for more practice with the vocabulary.
Practice > Unit 6 > Activity 3

C. IDENTIFY Circle the main idea of the article.

a. Lazy thinkers are more likely to make bad decisions about money and finances.

b. Some people have more lazy thoughts than others, but it is not their fault.

c. The lazy brain helps people save energy, but it can also cause bad decisions.

d. According to scientists, people are trying to save energy all the time.

D. CATEGORIZE Read the statements. Write *T* (true) or *F* (false). Then correct each false statement to make it true according to the article.

_____ 1. People have hundreds of lazy thoughts a day.

_____ 2. Lazy thinkers often believe things that are not true.

_____ 3. When people have lazy brains, they don't feel confident about their decisions.

_____ 4. The subjects in the experiment decided to change their pace.

_____ 5. Choosing a career is an example of hard thinking.

_____ 6. When people solve difficult math problems, they are using less energy.

_____ 7. One way to fight lazy thinking is to think faster.

E. EXPLAIN Answer the questions. Write the paragraph number where the answer is found.

1. What kind of thinking do people use when they drive? Paragraph: _____

   _____

2. Why does the brain make lazy decisions? Paragraph: _____

   _____

3. How is hard thinking different from lazy thinking? Paragraph: _____

   _____
   _____

4. What advice do scientists give about how to fight lazy thinking? Paragraph: _____

   _____
   _____

136   UNIT 6   Are you a good decision maker?

F. ANALYZE Read each situation. Check (✓) if you think the situation uses lazy thinking or hard thinking. Compare your answers with a partner.

	Lazy thinking	Hard thinking
1. driving to the store	☐	☐
2. reading a textbook	☐	☐
3. choosing a college	☐	☐
4. making coffee	☐	☐
5. buying milk at the store	☐	☐
6. multiplying 14 x 19	☐	☐
7. giving a friend advice	☐	☐
8. choosing a seat on the bus	☐	☐

G. DISCUSS Work with a partner. Make a list of decisions you made today. Which ones do you think were lazy? Which ones were not lazy?

iQ PRACTICE Go online for additional reading and comprehension.
Practice > Unit 6 > Activity 4

WRITE WHAT YOU THINK

A. DISCUSS Discuss the questions in a group. Think about the Unit Question, "Are you a good decision maker?"

1. Do you think you are a lazy thinker when you make decisions? Why or why not?

2. When did you make a decision using hard thinking? Was it a good decision?

3. When you meet someone new, can you tell if the person is honest or not? How?

B. COMPOSE Choose one of the questions from Activity A and write a paragraph in response. Look back at your Quick Write on page 132 as you think about what you learned.

READING SKILL Using a graphic organizer

Graphic organizers represent ideas with images, such as diagrams, charts, tables, and timelines. You can use graphic organizers to help you see connections between ideas or remember the main points of a text or parts of a text. Drawing graphic organizers can help you review a text you have read in preparation for class or a test.

Scientific articles often show cause-effect or reason-result relationships. This reason-result organizer shows the relationship between a reason and its different results.

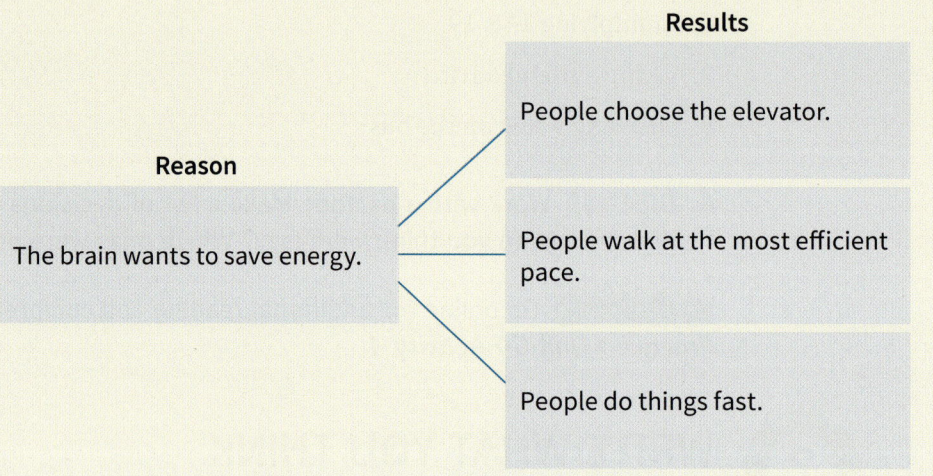

TIP FOR SUCCESS
Looking for patterns of organization in a text will help you understand what the writer wants to say about the topic.

A. CATEGORIZE Write the ideas from Reading 1 into the graphic organizer to illustrate the main reasons and results.

| People make bad decisions. | People have lazy thinking. |
| People feel too confident. | People believe things without proof. |

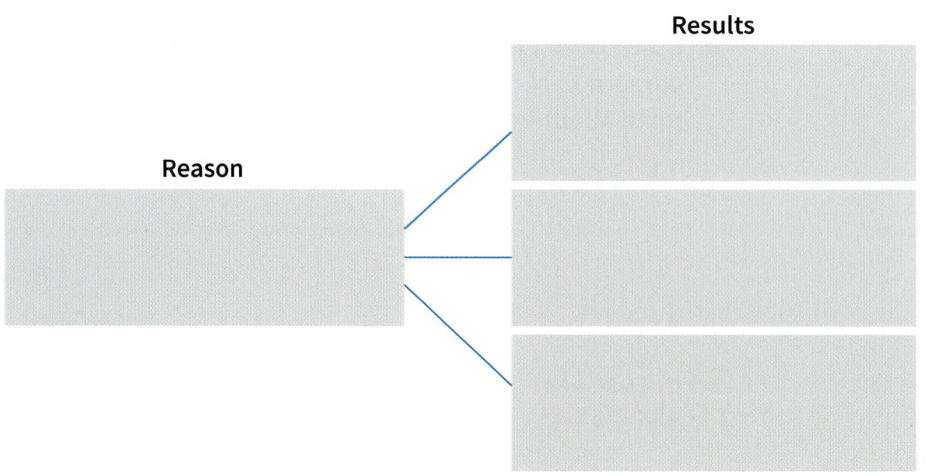

B. EXTEND Work with a partner. Read the paragraph from Reading 1. Make a reason-result graphic organizer to illustrate the main reason and its results.

When we use hard thinking, the body isn't so happy because we are demanding a lot more energy from it. That explains why students get so tired after studying for a test. It explains why long conversations make people want to grab a cup of coffee. They need the caffeine because they feel like they're out of energy. They're not using their lazy brain anymore.

iQ PRACTICE Go online for more practice with using a graphic organizer.
Practice > Unit 6 > Activity 5

READING 2

Problem-Solvers: Which One Are You?

OBJECTIVE ▶

You are going to read a magazine article about different ways people solve problems. Use the article to gather information and ideas for your Unit Assignment.

PREVIEW THE READING

A. PREVIEW Read the title of the article and skim the first two paragraphs. What is the purpose of the article? Check (✓) your answer.

☐ to explain how people solve problems in different ways

☐ to describe the kinds of problems people have at work

☐ to suggest why some people are more creative than others

B. QUICK WRITE When you have an assignment to do at school or work, do you prefer to work alone, in a small group, or in a big group? Why? Write for 5–10 minutes in response. Be sure to use this section for your Unit Assignment.

C. VOCABULARY Check (✓) the words you know. Then work with a partner to locate each word in the reading.

arrogant *(adj.)*	have a gift *(v. phr.)*	revolutionary *(adj.)*
come up with *(v. phr.)*	impatient *(adj.)* 🔑	view *(v.)* 🔑 OPAL
deal with *(v. phr.)*	move on *(v. phr.)*	

🔑 Oxford 3000™ words   **OPAL** Oxford Phrasal Academic Lexicon

iQ PRACTICE Go online to listen and practice your pronunciation.
Practice > Unit 6 > Activity 6

WORK WITH THE READING

 A. INVESTIGATE Read the article and gather information about how different kinds of people make decisions.

PROBLEM SOLVERS: WHICH ONE ARE YOU?

1. At school, at work, in life—you're always solving problems. How you solve a problem may be very different from the way others do. You might want to fix it quickly, but others want to take their time. You might have a lot of creative ideas, but you take a lot of time to make decisions.

2. The way people think about problems varies greatly. Everyone is unique, but psychologists believe there are about five different kinds of problem-solvers in the world. And knowing which one you are can have a big impact on your ability to work with other people successfully. So, which one sounds the most like you?

QUESTIONERS

3. Questioners are people who think hard about a problem. They ask many questions to themselves and to others. The more complex the problem is, the more questions they will ask about it. Sometimes they even answer people's questions with a question. They want to make sure they have thought about everything before making a decision. Questioners are good because their questions make other people think harder, too. But the problem is these problem-solvers can also be very slow to solve a problem.

IDEATORS

4. Ideators are the idea people. They're the most creative thinkers in the room. They can easily influence people because their ideas are so unique, and people are impressed by their minds. Because Ideators **have a gift**, their solutions can be truly **revolutionary**. The negative side is that they can sometimes annoy other people because they care less about finding a solution. They think of lots of solutions, and some of them may never work. So they're slower decision makers.

DIGGERS

5   Diggers are good to have on a team because they think about all the details. They want to "dig into" a problem and break it down so they can see all of the facts. When they have them all, then they can make their final decision. Consequently, they usually feel very confident about their choices. However, they can be slow at making decisions, and they may not offer their opinions to others until the very end. This can make other people wrongly assume that they aren't really working on the problem.

DOERS

6   For Doers, getting to a solution quickly is very important. They don't spend as much time asking questions or digging into problems. They prefer to focus on the present because they don't want to waste time thinking about the past. They try to keep things moving along in the right direction. Sometimes, Doers don't even wait to find the complete solution. For them, it's OK to just solve part of the problem and **move on**. So, Doers are excellent at solving things quickly, but sometimes other people see them as too **impatient**.

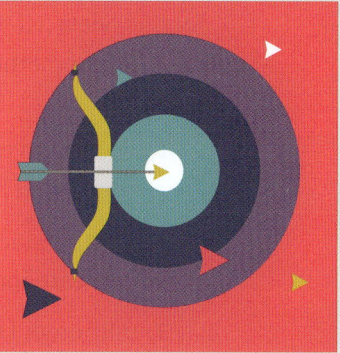

REASONERS

7   Reasoners are the people who like to keep things simple. When they **deal with** a complex problem, they prefer to focus on the most important elements. They don't want to worry about small details, which means they solve problems more quickly than other people. Also, for Reasoners, the "best" solution is the solution that they **came up with**. Unfortunately, they also have a hard time listening to other people's ideas. As a result, people sometimes see Reasoners as too confident or **arrogant**.

8   When you figure out what kind of problem-solver you are, you can understand how you think. Perhaps more importantly, you will also begin to see how other people **view** you. That is very important because teamwork is one of the most important skills people need to succeed in today's world. In college, students are constantly asked to work in groups and do team projects. At work, you'll be a part of many teams, and you'll need to come to solutions together. When you know the strengths and your weaknesses of your thinking, you will be able to work with others to solve problems even more successfully.

B. VOCABULARY Here are some words from Reading 2. Read the definitions. Then complete each sentence with the correct word.

arrogant *(adj.)* behaving in a proud or unpleasant way, showing little thought for other people
come up with *(v. phr.)* to find or produce an answer, a sum of money, etc.
deal with *(v. phr.)* to solve a problem, solve a task, etc.
have a gift *(v. phr.)* to be very good at doing something
impatient *(adj.)* annoyed or irritated by someone or something, especially because you have to wait for a long time
move on *(v. phr.)* to start doing or discussing something new
revolutionary *(adj.)* involving a great or complete change
view *(v.)* to have a personal opinion about or particular attitude toward something

1. John is a very _____ person. He always thinks he has the best ideas, and he never thinks he is wrong.

2. The president of the college had a(n) _____ idea to provide free day care for students with young children.

3. Although I was not very happy with my test results, I decided to _____ and begin thinking about how to do better on the next one.

4. Sometimes my coworker can be very _____. He has trouble waiting for things, and he prefers to get projects done early, even if they aren't perfect.

5. My mother and father _____ problems very differently. My father usually makes decisions on his own, but my mother prefers to ask friends for their advice first.

6. My daughters both _____ for the arts. One is a successful painter, and the other plays the violin in an orchestra.

7. Many people _____ the boss as someone you should listen to and not disagree with, but in my opinion, it's good to speak up when you have a different point of view.

8. Even though Sami is only 13, he has already _____ a plan to study medicine and become a doctor when he gets older.

iQ PRACTICE Go online for more practice with the vocabulary.
Practice > Unit 6 > Activity 7

C. IDENTIFY What is the main idea of the article? Circle the answer.

a. People are always solving problems in their lives, but some people take more time to solve problems than other people.

b. Understanding the personalities of different kinds of problem-solvers can help people be more successful when working with others.

c. Teamwork has become one of the most important skills in the workplace and at school because people always work in groups.

d. Reasoners and Doers prefer to solve problems slowly, but Diggers, Ideators, and Questioners take more time making decisions.

D. CATEGORIZE Read each set of positive and negative characteristics. Then write the type of problem-solver they describe.

Type of problem-solver	Positive characteristic	Negative characteristic
1.	They solve problems very quickly.	They can be impatient.
2.	They help other people think more.	They solve problems slower than others.
3.	They are able to see all the details of a problem.	They are slow to give their opinion about a solution.
4.	They are able to solve problems faster than others.	They can be seen as arrogant.
5.	They come up with ideas that no one else thinks about.	They can annoy people who want a real solution.

E. EVALUATE Look at the positive and negative characteristics of the five categories of people in Activity D. How are the types similar and different? With a partner, use the phrases below to state the similarities and differences.

(Questioners) and (Ideators) are similar because . . .

(Questioners) and (Ideators) are different because . . .

F. IDENTIFY Read these sentences from Reading 2. Then answer the questions. Find the sentences in the reading to help you.

1. (Paragraph 1) You might want to fix **it** quickly, but others want to take their time.

   What does *it* refer to? _____

2. (Paragraph 3) **They** want to make sure they have thought about everything before making a decision.

   Who does *they* refer to? _____

3. (Paragraph 4) **They** can easily influence people because their ideas are so unique.

   Who does *they* refer to? _____

4. (Paragraph 4) They think of lots of solutions, and some of **them** may never work.

   What does *them* refer to? _____

5. (Paragraph 5) When they have **them** all, then they can make their final decision.

   What does *them* refer to? _____

6. (Paragraph 6) For **them**, it's OK to just solve part of the problem and move on.

   Who does *them* refer to? _____

CRITICAL THINKING STRATEGY

Classifying information

When you **classify** information, you arrange ideas into different types or categories according to how they are similar to each other. For example, in Reading 2, the author classified people into five different problem-solving types to show what is special about each one. When you classify, you are better able to see similarities and differences among the categories.

iQ PRACTICE Go online to watch the Critical Thinking Video and check your comprehension. *Practice > Unit 6 > Activity 8*

G. CATEGORIZE Read about the different problem-solvers. Classify them according to the type of problem-solver they are. Go back to Reading 2 to help you.

_____ 1. Everybody loves Rodolfo! He has the most interesting ideas, and he's always thinking of new ways to do something. The only problem is sometimes he doesn't stay focused on the real problem.

_____ 2. Maryam is really good to have on our team because she helps us break down a problem into the smallest parts. Then each of us can work on a different detail at a time. Unfortunately, sometimes she can take a long time to figure out what those details are.

_____ 3. Norbert is the guy you want on your team if you want something done on time. In fact, he's so fast that he usually finishes his projects early! Norbert is good for me because sometimes I am just way too slow at completing a project.

_____ 4. Rushi is such a patient person! He will go over and over and over something until he finds the answer he's looking for. Sometimes I say to him, "Well, what do you think?" His response? "I know what I think, but what do _you_ think?"

_____ 5. Bridget is an interesting person. She's very smart, and she can deal with all kinds of problems, from simple to complex. However, she often doesn't really hear what other people are trying to say, and that can upset them.

H. COMPOSE What kind of problem-solver do you think like the most? Write a paragraph of 5–8 sentences in response.

WORK WITH THE VIDEO

A. PREVIEW Is it possible to know when something good or bad will happen before it happens? Share your opinion with a partner.

VIDEO VOCABULARY

crew (n.) all the people working on a ship, plane, firetruck, etc.

backdraft (n.) an explosion caused by more oxygen being supplied to a fire, for example, by a door being opened

intuition (n.) the feeling or understanding that makes you believe or know something without any reason or proof

subconsciously (adv.) connected with feelings that influence your behavior even though you are not aware of them

iQ RESOURCES Go online to watch the video about intuition.
Resources > Video > Unit 6 > Unit Video

B. IDENTIFY Watch the video two or three times. Then choose the correct answers.

1. Andy Kirk had a *normal / strange* feeling.
2. Andy told the firefighters to *enter / leave* the building.
3. The color of the smoke was *gray / orange*.
4. Air was rushing *out of / into* the building
5. There was *a lot of / no* sound from the fire.
6. Andy's *conscious / subconscious* mind saved people's lives.

C. EXTEND The video suggests that people can make good decisions to help others very quickly in an emergency situation. What is an example of a quick decision you've made that helped someone?

WRITE WHAT YOU THINK

SYNTHESIZE Think about Reading 1, Reading 2, and the unit video as you discuss these questions. Then choose one question and write a paragraph in response.

1. Think about a friend or family member who usually makes good decisions. Why do you think he or she is a good decision maker?

2. What are factors that can make people make bad decisions? Are they factors people can control or not control?

3. Do you think people generally think only one way, or is it possible for someone to think in many different ways?

VOCABULARY SKILL Phrasal verbs

A **phrasal verb** is a combination of a verb and a particle. Particles are usually prepositions, such as *up, on, in, down,* and *over*. When they are combined with a verb, however, they can change the meaning of the verb.

Compare these pairs of sentences:

> The company recently decided to **move** its main headquarters from Los Angeles to Toronto, Canada.
>
> When Jack finishes a project, he likes to **move on** right away to the next one so he doesn't waste time.
>
> According to the rules of the game, I had to **deal** everyone seven cards and place the rest of the cards on the table.
>
> When I have lots of things to do, I prefer to **deal with** the hardest thing first and then go on to the easier ones.

The phrasal verb *move on* has a different meaning from the verb *move*.

> move ➡ to change the place where you live or have your work
>
> move on ➡ to start doing or discussing something new

The phrasal verb *deal with* has a different meaning from the verb *deal*.

> deal ➡ to give cards to each player in a game of cards
>
> deal with ➡ to take action in order to solve a problem or complete a task

A. INTERPRET Match each phrasal verb with its definition below. Look back at the readings to help you.

___ 1. run into (Reading 1, Paragraph 6)

___ 2. end up (Reading 1, Paragraph 8)

___ 3. think through (Reading 1, Paragraph 8)

___ 4. break down (Reading 2, Paragraph 5)

___ 5. move along (Reading 2, Paragraph 6)

___ 6. figure out (Reading 2, Paragraph 8)

a. to think about something until you understand it

b. to find yourself in a place or situation that you did not intend or expect to be in

c. to experience problems

d. to keep something going

e. to separate things into parts in order to analyze it or make it easier to do

f. to consider a problem or a possible course of action fully

B. APPLY Complete each sentence with the correct phrasal verb from Activity A.

1. I want to complete the project by the end of the day, but I think I will _____ having to bring it home to finish it.

2. It was difficult for her to _____ the answer to the question because she didn't understand a lot of the vocabulary in the text.

3. My algebra teacher has the ability to _____ a complex math problem into smaller pieces so students can understand it better.

4. Some people _____ trouble when they make the wrong judgment about someone new they meet.

5. Doers want to make sure that things _____ quickly so that they can find a solution and not waste time.

6. The teenager didn't _____ all of the consequences of his actions. As a result, he made a big mistake and got into trouble with his parents.

iQ PRACTICE Go online for more practice with phrasal verbs.
Practice > Unit 6 > Activity 9

WRITING

OBJECTIVE ▶ At the end of this unit, you will write an analysis essay using reasons and examples about whether you're a good decision maker. This essay will include specific information from the readings, the unit video, and your own ideas.

WRITING SKILL Stating reasons and giving examples

An **analysis essay** is a piece of writing that carefully examines a topic by breaking it down into smaller parts. The writer looks at the smaller parts in separate body paragraphs and explains them so the reader will understand the main topic. To help explain the topic and pieces, the writer states reasons and gives examples.

Writers state **reasons** to explain why something happens or is true. Reasons can explain why people act or do things in a certain way or why things happen. Writers support their reasons with **examples**. Examples can be specific situations, observations, or personal experiences that writers give to make their reasons clear.

Thesis statement (situation): In my opinion, I think a lot like a Doer.

Topic sentence (Reason 1): One reason I'm a Doer is because I prefer to focus on the present.

Example: I try not to worry about past mistakes that I've made in my life.

Example: I don't think a lot about the future because it's impossible to predict what will happen.

Topic sentence (Reason 2): Another reason I'm a Doer is because I like to make decisions quickly.

Example: I don't like wasting hours shopping for the perfect piece of clothing.

Example: I always know exactly what I want when I go out to eat at restaurants.

There are certain phrases that signal examples, such as *for example* and *for instance*.

Stating reasons with *because*

Because is often used to show reasons why something happens or is true. When *because* is at the beginning of a sentence, a comma is put before the second subject-verb combination.

[reason: Because I spent more time with my grandmother,] [second subject-verb combination: I think the most like her.]

When *because* is in the middle of a sentence, no comma is used.

Our boss made a bad decision [reason: because he didn't consider all of the facts.]

A. WRITING MODEL Read the model analysis essay. Underline the thesis statement in paragraph 1 and the topic sentences in paragraphs 2–4.

My Mother, Myself

1   I have a very loving mother. When I was young, we spent a lot of time together because she quit her job after I was born. She taught me how to walk, how to read, and how to be a good and honest person. Now I am in college, and I appreciate all of the time I was able to spend with her. I know now that my mother has had a very big influence on the way I think. We think a lot alike in the way we question things, deal with mistakes, and make decisions.

2   One reason my mother and I are similar is because we are both Questioners. We are very curious about life, and we always want to know more. We are more likely to answer each other's questions with another question instead of an actual answer. For example, the other day, my mother asked me, "Do you think I should cut my hair short?" I responded, "Well, do you want shorter hair, or do you like your hair long?" I preferred her hair long, but I didn't tell her that. I wanted her to discover the answer herself. The questions we ask each other help us solve problems because we make each other really think about our decisions. With my mother, no question is ever a bad question.

3   Another reason I think like my mother is because we both think too much about the past. For instance, when I make a mistake, it is hard for me to forget about it. I usually think about what I did for a long time. I think about what I could have done better. For example, if I made someone upset, I think about what I could have said differently to not make him or her angry. I have a hard time getting over mistakes. The problem with this is that I sometimes can't focus on the present. For instance, when I am with my friends and we are having fun, I might still be thinking about a mistake I made earlier that day, but then I don't enjoy the experience as much. I definitely get this trait from my mother. She always worries about past mistakes even though she knows they can't be changed.

4   Finally, both my mother and I are slow when it comes to making important decisions. Because we're both natural Diggers, we both like to think things through for a long time before we decide to take action. For example, I recently moved out from my parents' house, and I had to decide what kind of apartment to get. I didn't want to just take the first one I saw. In fact, I looked at over 15 apartments before I decided on the one. I had to get all the facts: the price, the size, the neighborhood. Then I had to compare everything to choose the best apartment. My mother was with me the whole time, and she was digging through the facts just as much as I was. This meant that it took a little long to finally decide, but in the end, we were both confident about my decision.

5   All in all, there are a lot of reasons why I think like my mother. Because we're both Questioners and Diggers, we help each other think more deeply about life. However, nobody is perfect, and we both struggle sometimes with thinking too much in the past and not focusing enough on the present. Still, I am very proud to carry on the same thinking that my mother has given me. We are definitely not lazy thinkers, and that's probably why we've both been able to lead happy, successful lives.

B. CATEGORIZE Complete the graphic organizer with information from the essay in Activity A.

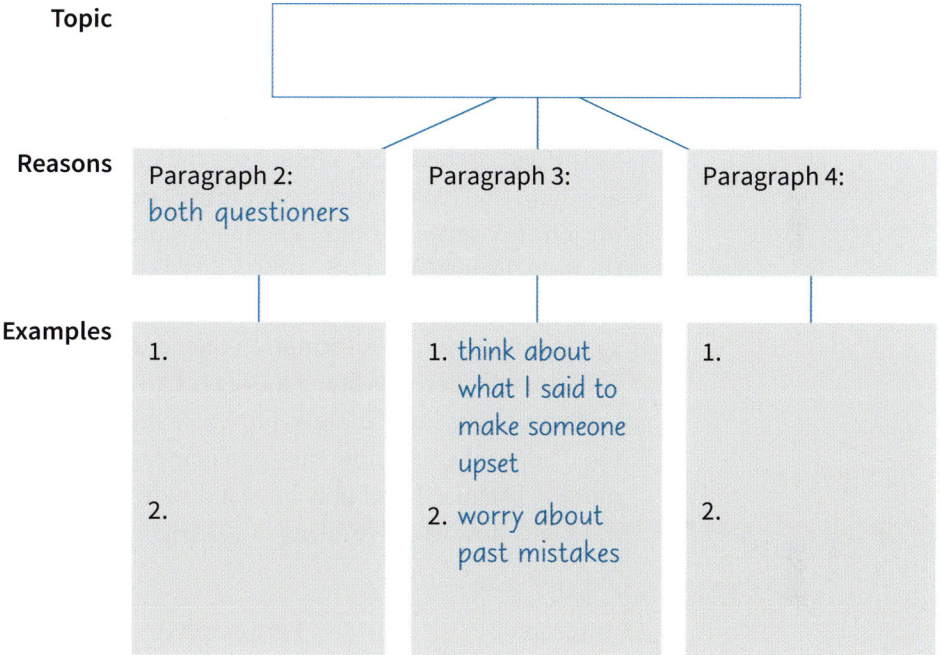

C. WRITING MODEL Read the model analysis essay. On page 152, match the examples with the reason in each body paragraph.

Being a Digger

1   I have always loved numbers. I am an accountant, and I currently work for a large bank in Toronto, Canada. I work with a team of about 20 people, and all of us bring something different to the table. We all have our own personalities, and we don't all solve problems the same way. When I think about how I solve problems, I definitely consider myself a Digger.

2   One reason I'm a Digger is because I'm very detail-oriented. For example, when I am with my coworkers, I am listening to what everyone is saying and writing down all the important points. Later, I go back and

review my notes to make sure I have everything. If I am missing any information, I will go back to the person to get it because I want all the facts. Sometimes this annoys people because they think that I wasn't really listening to them.

3   Another reason I'm a Digger is because I don't give my opinions right away. When I am in a meeting at work, I do not talk as much as other people. I will only speak up when I'm totally confident about what I have to say. I don't want to waste people's time just telling them the first thing that comes to my mind. I also like to think about what people are saying and reflect on that, so I usually don't always give my opinions at meetings. This doesn't mean I never share them, however. Often, I will talk to people later to give them my reflections and explain how I feel.

4   Finally, I'm a Digger because I am slow at making decisions. At work, people always want things fast. Every morning, we receive an email from our boss telling us all the things that need to be completed that day and by the end of the week. When I see the list, I can get a little nervous. It's not that I don't start working on things right away. I work hard and I take my job very seriously, but I just need more time to think because I need things to be perfect.

5   All in all, I think I'm definitely a Digger. I like to break problems down so that I have all the information I need to share my opinions or make decisions. Sometimes being a Digger can annoy my coworkers who like to solve problems immediately, but I also recognize that it has its strengths, too. People always know they can come to me for information they're missing because I probably have it down somewhere. And if I don't have it, I know how to dig for it.

____ Paragraph 2   ____ Paragraph 3   ____ Paragraph 4

a. For example, I can't even send a coworker an email until I am sure that it says exactly what I'm thinking.

b. For example, last week my coworker got a little upset with me for asking for the same information again, but I just wanted to be sure I understood it.

c. For example, I often email my coworkers the day after a meeting to share my opinion about how to solve a problem.

D. **IDENTIFY** Read the sentences. Underline the reasons. Add commas if needed.

1. Because Diggers get all of the facts they feel more confident about their decisions.

2. Because the businesspeople made bad decisions their companies lost a lot of money.

3. The scientists performed an experiment because they wanted to prove their theory.

4. Hard thinking takes more energy because the brain is working a lot more.

5. Because the subjects were using lazy thinking they changed their pace without knowing.

6. Reasoners are good to have on a team because they can help solve problems quickly.

iQ PRACTICE Go online for more practice with stating reasons and giving examples. *Practice > Unit 6 > Activity 10*

GRAMMAR Gerunds and infinitives

A **gerund** is the base form of a **verb + -ing**. Gerunds can function as nouns in a sentence. A gerund can be one word (*running, eating, living*) or part of a phrase (*running outdoors, eating healthily, living in a big city*).

Gerunds as subjects

A **gerund** or **gerund phrase** can be the subject of a sentence. A gerund subject always takes a singular verb.

Thinking <u>is</u> easier and faster when we use our lazy brain.

Being lazy <u>doesn't</u> just <u>mean</u> you take the elevator instead of the stairs.

Gerunds after verbs

Gerunds follow certain verbs. Here are some of the verbs that gerunds follow.

| avoid | discuss | enjoy | go | quit |
| consider | dislike | finish | practice | suggest |

An **infinitive** is *to* + **the base form** of a verb. Infinitives can function as objects in sentences.

Doers want **to solve** a problem as quickly as possible.

Infinitives follow certain verbs. Here are some of the verbs that infinitives follow.

| agree | decide | hope | plan | wait |
| appear | forget | learn | seem | want |

iQ RESOURCES Go online to watch the Grammar Skill Video.
Resources > Video > Unit 6 > Grammar Skill Video

A. COMPOSE Complete each sentence with a gerund phrase. Use the words in parentheses.

1. _Understanding human behavior_ (understand/human behavior) is not always easy.
2. _____ (be/a good listener) is a very important skill to have.
3. _____ (use/lazy thinking) can cause people to make bad decisions.
4. _____ (get/enough sleep) is crucial to your brain's health.
5. _____ (solve/complex problems) takes more time and effort.

B. APPLY Complete each sentence with a verb + a gerund. Use the words in parentheses.

1. I want to be healthier, but I really _dislike exercising_ (dislike/exercise).
2. If you have heart problems, you should _____ (quit/eat) salty foods.
3. Ahmed _____ (consider/move) to Riyadh, but he decided to stay in Jeddah.
4. We should _____ (avoid/buy) a big car because gasoline is too expensive.
5. Today we will _____ (discuss/write) paragraphs.
6. After Margo _____ (finish/eat) dinner, she read the newspaper.

C. APPLY Complete each sentence with a gerund or an infinitive. Use the verb in parentheses.

1. I hope ____to go____ (go) to Australia someday.
2. Yuri wants _____ (visit) his friend in Seoul next fall.
3. You should practice _____ (speak) Spanish every day.
4. My neighbor agreed _____ (help) me fix my car.
5. Do you enjoy _____ (play) soccer?
6. Jamal goes _____ (swim) every morning with his son.

iQ PRACTICE Go online for more practice with gerunds and infinitives.
Practice > Unit 6 > Activities 11–12

UNIT ASSIGNMENT Write an analysis essay with reasons and examples

OBJECTIVE ▶

In this assignment, you are going to write an analysis essay using reasons and examples. As you prepare to write, think about the Unit Question, "Are you a good decision maker?" Use information from Reading 1, Reading 2, the unit video, and your work in this unit to support your paragraph. Refer to the Self-Assessment checklist on page 156.

iQ RESOURCES Go online to the Writing Tutor to read a model analysis essay. *Practice › Unit 6 › Activity 13*

PLAN AND WRITE

A. BRAINSTORM Follow these steps to help you organize your ideas.

1. Think about the ways you make decisions about things that have happened in your life. Brainstorm reasons why you make good or bad decisions.

2. Brainstorm examples for your reasons in Step 1. Think about example situations and personal observations you can use to make your reasons clearer.

3. Think about the readings and video in this unit. Is there any information that can help support your ideas?

B. PLAN Write a thesis statement for your analysis essay.

iQ RESOURCES Go online to download and complete the outline for your analysis essay. *Resources › Writing Tools › Unit 6 › Outline*

C. WRITE Use your planning notes to write your essay.

1. Write your analysis essay that explains how you make decisions. Be sure to use reasons and examples to support your thesis statement.

2. Look at the Self-Assessment checklist on page 156 to guide your writing.

iQ PRACTICE Go online to the Writing Tutor to write your assignment. *Practice › Unit 6 › Activity 14*

REVISE AND EDIT

iQ RESOURCES Go online to download the peer review worksheet.
Resources > Writing Tools > Unit 6 > Peer Review Worksheet

A. PEER REVIEW Read your partner's essay. Then use the peer review worksheet. Discuss the review with your partner.

B. REWRITE Based on your partner's review, revise and rewrite your essay.

C. EDIT Complete the Self-Assessment checklist as you prepare to write the final draft of your essay. Be prepared to hand in your work or discuss it in class.

SELF-ASSESSMENT	Yes	No
Does the introductory paragraph include a thesis statement?	☐	☐
Does the essay include a body paragraph for each reason?	☐	☐
Does the essay contain examples to support the reasons?	☐	☐
Is *because* used correctly to state reasons? Are commas used if necessary?	☐	☐
Are gerunds with *-ing* forms used correctly?	☐	☐
Are all gerund subjects followed by a singular verb?	☐	☐
Does the essay contain phrasal verbs from the unit? Are they used correctly?	☐	☐
Does the essay include vocabulary from the unit?	☐	☐
Did you check the essay for grammar, punctuation, and spelling?	☐	☐

D. REFLECT Discuss these questions with a partner or group.

1. What is something new you learned in this unit?
2. Look back at the Unit Question—Are you a good decision maker? Is your answer different now than it was when you started the unit? If yes, how is it different? Why?

iQ PRACTICE Go to the online discussion board to discuss the questions.
Practice > Unit 6 > Activity 15

TRACK YOUR SUCCESS

iQ PRACTICE Go online to check the words and phrases you have learned in the unit. *Practice > Unit 6 > Activity 16*

Check (✓) the skills and strategies you learned. If you need more work on a skill, refer to the page(s) in parentheses.

READING	☐ I can use a graphic organizer. (p. 138)
CRITICAL THINKING	☐ I can classify information. (p. 144)
VOCABULARY	☐ I can use phrasal verbs. (p. 147)
WRITING	☐ I can state reasons and give examples. (p. 149)
GRAMMAR	☐ I can use gerunds and infinitives. (p. 153)
OBJECTIVE ▶	☐ I can gather information and ideas to write an analysis essay about whether I'm a good decision maker.

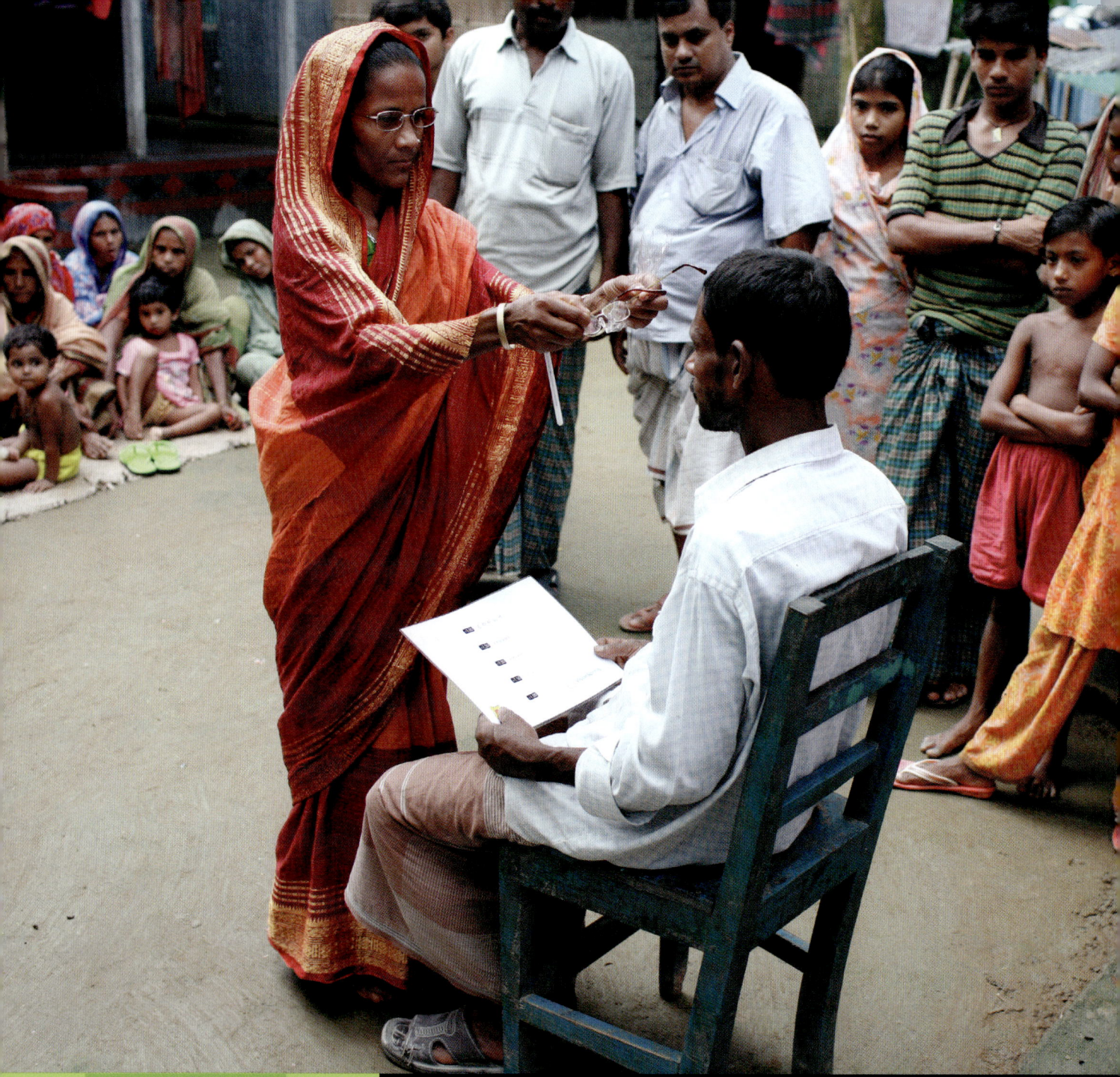

Economics

READING	using a timeline
CRITICAL THINKING	adding details to support statements
VOCABULARY	collocations with verbs
WRITING	writing a cause/effect essay
GRAMMAR	complex sentences

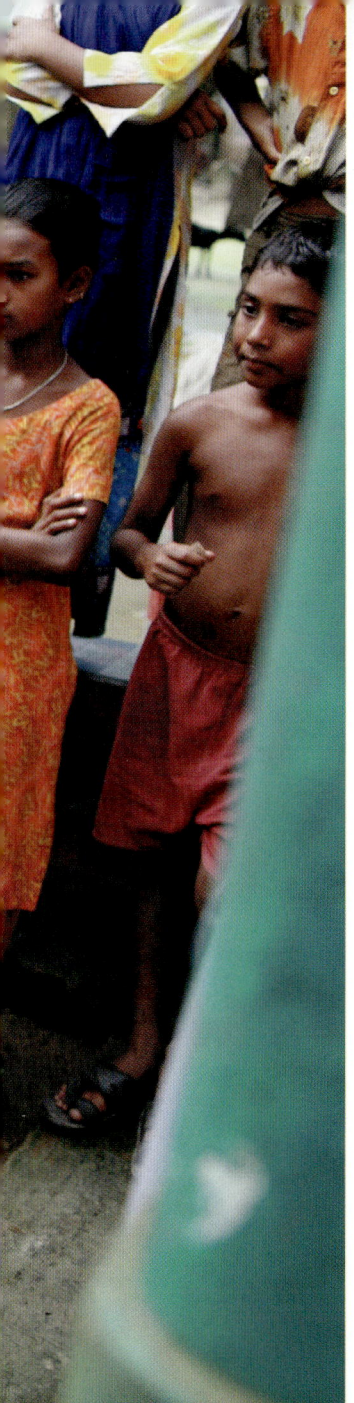

UNIT QUESTION

Can a business earn money while making a difference?

A. Discuss these questions with your classmates.

1. Have you ever thought about starting your own business? If yes, what kind of business would you like to have?

2. When you buy something, do you think about the company that you are purchasing from? For example, are you curious about where and how the products are made?

3. Look at the photo. What product do you think is being sold here?

B. Listen to *The Q Classroom* online. Then answer these questions.

1. Felix thinks that companies can earn money while making a difference. But he thinks it's important to have a good business plan. Do you agree? What kind of product or service can you imagine writing a business plan for?

2. Yuna says that she supports companies that have a social component. She wants the companies to succeed. How do you feel about this? Do you ever buy products because you know the company is doing something for the community?

iQ PRACTICE Go to the online discussion board to discuss the Unit Question with your classmates. *Practice > Unit 7 > Activity 1*

UNIT OBJECTIVE

Read the articles and gather information and ideas to write a cause/effect essay about how a business can make money while making a difference.

READING

READING 1

FEED Projects: How a Bag Can Feed Children in Many Ways

OBJECTIVE ▶ You are going to read a magazine article about social entrepreneurship, or a business that earns money and also makes a difference in the world. Use the article to gather information and ideas for your Unit Assignment.

PREVIEW THE READING

A. PREVIEW Read the title. How do you think this company will feed children?

B. QUICK WRITE Think about successful businesses. How do they earn money? What could they do with some of their profits to help others? Write for 5–10 minutes in response. Remember to use this section for your Unit Assignment.

C. VOCABULARY Check (✓) the words you know. Then work with a partner to locate each word in the reading. Use clues to help define the words you don't know. Check your definitions in the dictionary.

desire (n.) OPAL	massive (adj.)	reusable (adj.)
distribute (v.) OPAL	opportunity (n.) OPAL	signify (v.)
estimate (v.) OPAL	overall (adj.) OPAL	
firsthand (adv.)	prospect (n.)	

Oxford 3000™ words   OPAL Oxford Phrasal Academic Lexicon

iQ PRACTICE Go online to listen and practice your pronunciation.
Practice > Unit 7 > Activity 2

WORK WITH THE READING

 A. INVESTIGATE Read the article and gather information about how a business earns money while making a difference.

Lauren Bush Lauren giving a schoolchild a meal

FEED Projects:

How a Bag Can Feed Children in Many Ways

1   In 2004, when Lauren Bush Lauren was in college, she was a volunteer for the UN World Food Programme (WFP). This gave her the **opportunity** to travel to various countries around the world. She traveled to countries like Chad in Africa and Guatemala in Central America. In her travels, she saw **firsthand** the hunger that exists in many parts of the world. More significantly, she saw how hunger affects children. She also saw how important a school lunch was to these children. As she told a reporter for *Forbes*, " . . . a free school meal not only nourishes a child, but it provides a reason for them to go to school every day and stay in school longer. This means opportunity for equal education and better job **prospects**. While traveling with the WFP, I've witnessed how the school lunch is truly a community event. The mothers who come to help prepare the meal are able to eat, as well as their other children who are not yet school-aged."

2   Bush Lauren was affected by what she had seen, and she wanted to do something to help. After graduating from college in 2005, she kept thinking about how to help those children. Always interested in fashion and design, she came up with a way to combine her interest in design and her **desire** to help feed hungry children. She would create a bag to raise money for feeding the hungry.

3   At that time, **reusable** bags were becoming popular. Bush Lauren realized that if she designed a bag that could be reused, people might be interested in buying it. They might be more interested if they knew that their purchase would help feed hungry children. She partnered with Ellen Gustafson, who worked for the WFP at the time, and in 2007, FEED Projects was born.

4   That first bag was made of all natural products and looked similar to the bags that the UN had used to **distribute** food. It also had the number 1 on it. That number **signified** one year of school lunches a child would receive from that purchase. FEED worked with the WFP to distribute the meals to children in schools. Consumers knew that their purchase of the bag meant that a child would receive a meal every day for a year.

5   This was the first of many bags in the social business FEED. The bags became very popular and the company grew. Bush Lauren continued to design more bags with numbers on them signifying the number of school lunches that would be provided for each bag purchased. A percentage of the retail price of the bags sold is spent on feeding the hungry. This money then goes to organizations like the WFP to distribute the meals.

6   The impact of feeding the hungry is very powerful. Today over 795 million people are affected by hunger around the world. It has been

shown that when children are given a nutritious meal, they perform better in school. Their education improves, giving them a better chance of improving their lives. Providing nutrition improves not only the child's education, but also their **overall** health. Malnutrition, or not getting the right nutrition to meet your body's needs, is a major cause of disease and illness globally. By providing a child with one meal a day, malnutrition is greatly reduced.

7   It should be noted that hunger is not just a problem in developing countries. It is also a problem in the United States, where it is **estimated** that 42 million Americans lack food. In 2013, FEED started a program with the organization Feeding America to provide nutritious school lunches to children in poor communities in the United States.

8   FEED has continued to expand and grow. Today the company produces many different bags in different materials. Their products also include jewelry and scarves. Many of these products are made by local artisans, thus providing employment for people in those countries. Currently FEED provides meals in 63 countries, in Africa and Central America, as well as in the United States. In 2017, the first FEED cafe and shop opened in Brooklyn, New York. As of 2018, FEED had provided more than 100 million lunches to children.

9   The problem of world hunger can't be solved overnight, but FEED has taken small but noticeable steps. As Bush Lauren said, "Global hunger . . . can seem like a **massive** problem, but I started FEED because I hoped that by providing people with a . . . way to make a difference, they would be able to better understand the problem and participate in the solution . . . I've learned that people want to get involved . . . They just aren't always sure where to begin." And through FEED, she has given them a way to start.

ACADEMIC LANGUAGE

The corpus shows that *it has been shown that* is often used in academic writing.

OPAL
Oxford Phrasal Academic Lexicon

B. VOCABULARY Here are some words from Reading 1. Read the sentences. Then write each bold word next to the correct definition on page 163.

1. The **opportunity** to learn about business was very exciting to her.

2. His **overall** experience working at the marketing company was good, but he wanted to explore other work options.

3. I bought a bottle that is **reusable**. It's important to me to not create more waste.

4. When you have an internship, you can experience **firsthand** what it's like to work at a company.

5. The wildfire became **massive**, extending for more than 30,000 acres of the forest.

6. She achieved excellent grades in college, so the **prospect** of her getting a job was good.

7. The United Nations and other organizations **estimate** that over a billion people today live in poverty.

8. Many young people today have the **desire** to work in companies that give back to the community in some way.

9. Sali will have a performance review next week. This will **signify** whether she is doing well at her job or not.

10. Non-government organizations **distribute** food and medicine to people in need around the world.

a. _____ (v.) to transport or supply something to various people or places

b. _____ (v.) to calculate the size, cost, etc., of something

c. _____ (v.) to be a sign of something; to mean

d. _____ (n.) the feeling of wanting something very much; a strong wish

e. _____ (n.) a chance to do something you would like to do

f. _____ (n.) a chance or hope that something will happen

g. _____ (adj.) heard, seen, or learned directly, not from other people

h. _____ (adj.) very big

i. _____ (adj.) including everything

j. _____ (adj.) that can be used again

iQ PRACTICE Go online for more practice with the vocabulary.
Practice > Unit 7 > Activity 3

C. IDENTIFY Read the main ideas. Write the paragraph number where they are found.

____ 1. Lauren Bush Lauren found an idea for combining her love of fashion and her desire to help the hungry.

____ 2. The bag with the number 1 on it was the first bag that FEED made.

____ 3. After traveling with the UN WFP, Bush Lauren saw how important a school lunch was to hungry children.

____ 4. FEED also works in the United States, where there are many hungry people.

____ 5. Bush Lauren founded her business because she wanted to give people a way to help solve the problem of hunger.

____ 6. Providing a school lunch has a great impact on a child, such as improving their health.

D. CATEGORIZE Read the statements. Write *T* (true) or *F* (false). Then correct each false statement to make it true according to the article.

___ 1. Lauren Bush Lauren traveled to countries around the world with the UN World Food Programme after she graduated from college.

___ 2. A free meal helps children stay in school.

___ 3. The first bag designed for FEED had the number 1 on it signifying one lunch for a child in need.

___ 4. A percentage of the profits from the sale of bags goes to feeding hungry children.

___ 5. FEED distributes meals to schoolchildren in 63 countries of the world.

___ 6. The company has expanded and now includes items like scarves and shoes.

E. INTERPRET Look more closely at the reading and answer the following questions. Write the sentence(s) that provide the answers.

1. What are other ways that a free school meal can "feed" children, according to the article?

   _____
   _____

2. In what ways can a school lunch be a "community event"?

   _____
   _____

3. Many founders of organizations have what is called an *aha moment* when they finally come up with an idea that they have been thinking about for a long time. What was Bush Lauren's aha moment?

   _____
   _____

4. Give an example of the global impact of feeding children.

   _____
   _____

F. EXTEND Look back at your Quick Write on page 160. Can you think of other products a company might sell to earn money and do good? Add any new ideas or information you learned from the reading.

iQ PRACTICE Go online for additional reading and comprehension.
Practice › Unit 7 › Activity 4

WRITE WHAT YOU THINK

A. DISCUSS Discuss the questions in a group. Think about the Unit Question, "Can a business earn money while making a difference?"

1. Lauren Bush Lauren saw a need that she felt passionate about. Is there any global problem that you feel passionate about?

2. Many social enterprises are able to fund their social cause by charging more for their products. Do you think this is a good way to raise money? Would you pay more to buy a product because it has a social impact?

B. CREATE Choose one of the questions from Activity A and write a paragraph in response. Look back at your Quick Write on page 160 as you think about what you learned.

READING SKILL Using a timeline

Creating a **timeline** can be useful for understanding and remembering the events in a text. A timeline should show all of the important events that happened during a period of time. Look at the timeline for Reading 1.

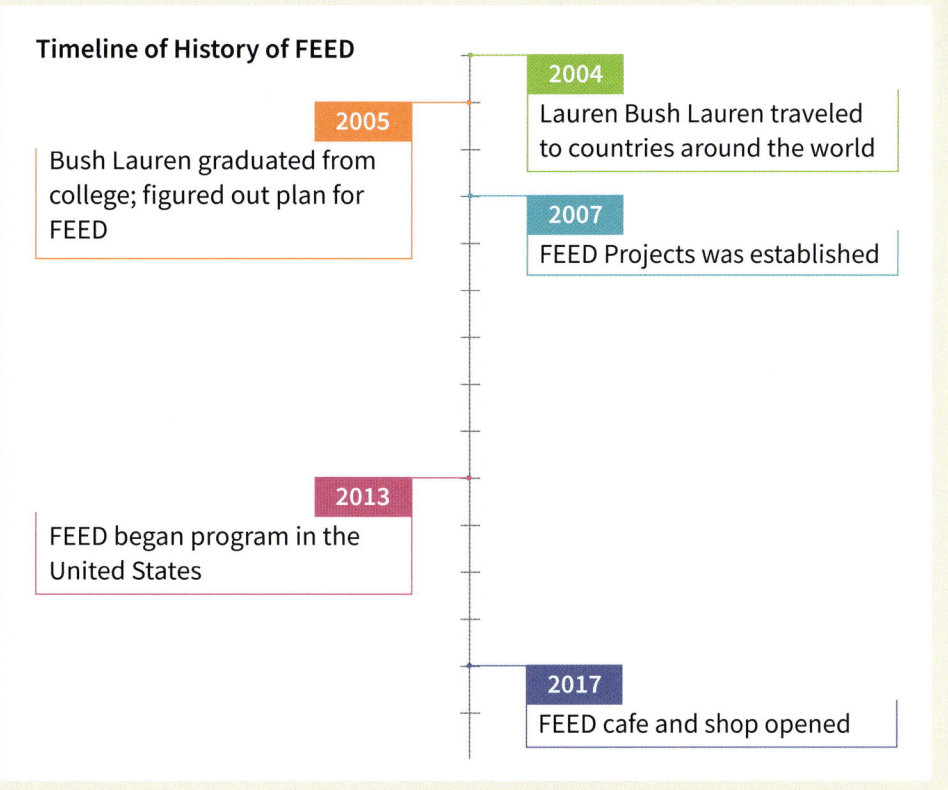

iQ RESOURCES Go online to watch the Reading Skill Video.
Resources > Video > Unit 7 > Reading Skill Video

A. INVESTIGATE Read the article. Then complete the timeline. Use the sentences from the box.

Did you know that spending a few dollars on a bottle of salad dressing can help children with serious illnesses enjoy a week at summer camp? It's true, thanks to Newman's Own.

In December 1980, Paul Newman, a well-known American film actor, and his friend A.E. Hotchner made gallons of salad dressing to give to family and friends as gifts. Their friends loved it and wanted more, so Newman and Hotchner made more. But this time, they decided to bottle it and sell it. And the rest, as they say, is history. Newman's Own was born.

By the end of 1982, the first year of production, the profits were close to $400,000. It was a hit! Since neither Newman nor Hotchner needed money, Newman said, "Let's give it all away to those who need it." Over the years Newman's Own added different kinds of products. Newman died in 2008, but his business still carries on with 100 percent of the profits donated to charities. By the end of 2018, there were over 300 products sold, and more than $500 million had been donated to charities.

The company donates to various charities, but the one perhaps closest to Newman's heart is the Hole in the Wall Gang camp, founded in 1988. This special camp is designed specifically for seriously ill children. For one week, these children can forget about their illnesses and enjoy themselves. Their medical needs are taken care of, and since they are all sick, the children don't have to feel "different." Because of Newman's Own Foundation, all of this is provided free for the campers. It's all paid for by people buying salad dressing—a small price for such a great reward.

The Hole in the Wall Gang camp was founded.
Paul Newman died.
Newman and Hotchner made salad dressing for gifts.
More than 300 products were sold.
Profits were close to $400,000.

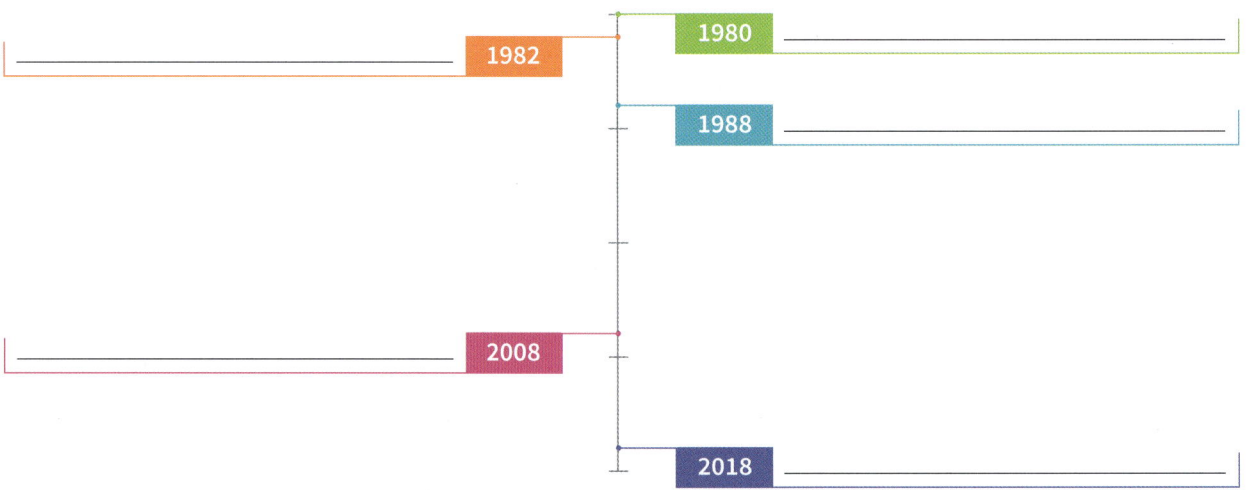

iQ PRACTICE Go online for more practice with using a timeline.
Practice > Unit 7 > Activity 5

READING 2

A New Business Model: Do Well While Doing Good

OBJECTIVE ▶

You are going to read an article from a business magazine about how businesses can earn money and do good. Use the article to gather information and ideas for your Unit Assignment.

PREVIEW THE READING

A. PREVIEW Look at the title and headings. What do you think the article is going to tell us about businesses that want to help others? Check (✓) your answer.

☐ Companies are having a hard time making money while helping others.

☐ Consumers are interested in the kinds of products social enterprises offer.

☐ Entrepreneurs have figured out ways to help others by doing more than just donating goods.

B. QUICK WRITE Why do businesses want to help others? Are consumers different today than in previous times? Write for 5–10 minutes in response. Be sure to use this section for your Unit Assignment.

C. VOCABULARY Check (✓) the words you know. Use a dictionary to define any new or unknown words. Then discuss how the words will relate to the unit with a partner.

address *(v.)* OPAL	focus *(n.)* OPAL	model *(n.)* OPAL
aspect *(n.)* OPAL	give back *(v. phr.)*	movement *(n.)* OPAL
concerned *(adj.)* OPAL	inspired *(adj.)*	seek *(v.)* OPAL

Oxford 3000™ words   OPAL Oxford Phrasal Academic Lexicon

iQ PRACTICE Go online to listen and practice your pronunciation.
Practice > Unit 7 > Activity 6

WORK WITH THE READING

 A. INVESTIGATE Read the article and gather information about how businesses can earn money and do good.

Home   Sign in

ABOUT   LATEST POSTS   ARCHIVES   SUBSCRIBE

A NEW BUSINESS MODEL: DO WELL WHILE DOING GOOD

1   In the business world today, there is a growing **movement** to include a social component in a company's business plan. More and more young entrepreneurs feel the need to **give back** to the community in some way, and they've included this **aspect** in the companies that they are establishing.

Why the change?

2   Some say that it's the young people who feel differently about their futures. They don't want their work to be just about making money. Many young business people feel the desire to help others while fulfilling their own dreams of having a successful company.

3   And they've seen other successful stories to guide them, for example, lifestyle brand TOMS started in 2006. This is a company that was established on the principle of "One for One®." This means that when you purchase one of their products—for example, shoes—the company will donate a new pair to a child in need. So the company is based on a principle in which it has a product that earns them money but also allows them to give back to people. As of 2018, it employed around 500 employees and gave away 86 million pairs of shoes, provided 600,000 sight restorations, and helped secure 600,000 weeks of safe water to many communities around the world.

4   Many consumers also like the idea of giving back to the community. In a recent survey, 66 percent of people said they would pay more for an item if the company was doing social good with their purchases. It makes consumers feel good because they are indirectly helping someone in need by their purchase.

Children in TOMS shoes

From footwear to eyeglasses

5   It's not just a simple product that is the **focus** of these social ventures. Another company, Warby Parker, sells eyeglasses. They also help people in developing countries to see better. Using the one-for-one **model**, Warby Parker donates a pair of eyeglasses for every pair of Warby Parker eyeglasses purchased. (As of 2018, 2 million pairs of glasses had been donated. The company is valued at $1.75 billion.) In addition to eyeglasses, the company works with partners both in the U.S. and in developing countries that provide vision tests and glasses for children and adults. One of their

partners, VisionSpring, has provided vision tests and eyeglasses to millions of people around the world. The impact of all of this is easy to see. When a person's vision is improved, he or she will be able to learn better in school or be able to get a job and work better. This improves life for individuals and the overall economy of a particular area.

Nokero lights

How it works

6   With most social enterprises, there is a legitimate business of selling either goods or services. These companies are clearly for-profit businesses. From the profits of the goods sold, the company is able to donate goods or services to others around the world. Very often, the price of the goods bought is much higher than the goods provided, but as has been noted, people are willing to pay more for a product or service if they know that this is benefiting society in some way. The important difference between for-profit and social businesses is that the social give-back element is built into the business model of social entrepreneurship. You could say it's part of its DNA.

Different models

7   Some companies do not necessarily donate goods, but focus on global issues, such as the environment. One company, Nokero, has invented and produces very efficient solar lights. The name of the company means *no kerosene*. The company's mission is to eliminate the use of kerosene around the world. There are an estimated 1.2 billion people in the world that have no electricity. They rely on kerosene for both cooking and lighting. Kerosene is a very dangerous material, easily causing fires. It is also a major pollutant of the air. Nokero tries to **address** this problem. It provides people with an alternative to kerosene. They sell their lights to NGOs[1] at greatly reduced prices. The NGOs then distribute the lights to areas of need. The company tries to solve a global problem, but also is profitable. In 2015, it had earned $2 million in revenue.

8   Another environmental social venture is United by Blue. The company was started by a scuba diver who was **concerned** about the growing amount of plastic and other garbage in the oceans. He started a clothing company, and for each purchase, the company will clean a pound of garbage from "the world's oceans and waterways." To date, the company has cleaned over a million pounds of garbage from the water.

What they have in common

9   All of the founders of these social enterprises have a few qualities in common. First, they saw a problem and thought of a creative way to address it. Second, they are enthusiastic, even passionate about their cause. In addition, they are determined to make their company work. To this end, they **seek** experienced people to help them meet their goals. And finally, social entrepreneurs feel **inspired** by their work, especially when they see the results of their efforts firsthand. This is probably what keeps them, and their companies, going.

[1]**NGO:** non-government organization

B. VOCABULARY Complete the paragraph with the vocabulary from Reading 2. You may need to change the form of some of the words.

address (v.)	focus (n.)	model (n.)
aspect (n.)	give back (v. phr.)	movement (n.)
concerned (adj.)	inspired (adj.)	seek (v.)

I recently read about a company that is a social enterprise. I went to the store to buy some cleaning products. I was _____1_____ about all of the chemicals listed on the back of some of these products. Then I saw a product that claimed to be free of such ingredients. When I got home, I looked up the company on the Internet. It seems that the company was established by two college friends who were also _____2_____ natural cleaning products. Their story is quite interesting. They started making the products in their bathtub. After selling some of the products on the Internet, they started this company that has as its _____3_____ the elimination of chemicals from the environment. Their business _____4_____ has a social _____5_____ built into it. They want to eliminate toxic products from the environment. Through their company, they are making a small dent in doing so. They were one of the earlier businesses involved in a growing _____6_____ to do social good. They _____7_____ the issue of climate change by creating "green" products. They have even constructed their latest office in the greenest possible way. I feel _____8_____ by their story and hope I can use my skills to start a company that can also _____9_____ to society.

iQ PRACTICE Go online for more practice with the vocabulary.
Practice > Unit 7 > Activity 7

C. **APPLY** Complete the statements from Reading 2. Circle the correct answer.

1. In paragraph 5, line 1, the word *ventures* most likely means ___.
   a. new businesses
   b. trips
   c. products

2. In the last line of paragraph 5, the word *this* refers to ___.
   a. the amount of money the company earns
   b. getting cheap eyeglasses
   c. providing vision tests and eyeglasses to millions of people

3. in paragraph 3, line 8, *give back* most likely means ___.
   a. return
   b. provide help
   c. get money

4. In paragraph 7, line 6, *this problem* refers to ___.
   a. how kerosene is dangerous and pollutes the air
   b. not enough food
   c. not enough water

5. Look back at the title of the article. *Do Well* most likely means ___.
   a. start a business
   b. be successful
   c. get a job

6. *Doing Good* most likely means ___.
   a. helping others
   b. earning money
   c. being successful

D. IDENTIFY Complete the main ideas from Reading 2. Use the phrases from the box.

> has donated millions of shoes to people in need
> feel inspired to continue
> like the idea of giving back
> provide light and reduce pollution
> make a difference in the world
> is built into their business model

1. One of the reasons that the business model has changed is that many consumers _____.

2. Young business people feel differently about making money and want to _____.

3. TOMS is an example of a for-profit business that _____.

4. The difference between for-profit companies and social businesses is that in social enterprises, the social give-back element _____.

5. Nokero produces efficient solar lights which they sell at reduced prices to NGOs and, in this way, can _____.

6. One quality of social entrepreneurs is that when they see the results of their work, they _____.

E. CATEGORIZE Complete the chart with the information from the box: the problem or situation that the business founders saw, what they sell, and the effect or result.

pollution in oceans ~~shoes~~ ~~poor people have shoes~~
people can't see/ clothes cleaner oceans and waterways
   vision problems eyeglasses people have light after dark;
pollution and fires solar lights   less danger/pollution
~~kids have no shoes~~ people get glasses/
   have better vision

	Problem/Situation	What they sell	Effect/Result
1. TOMS	kids have no shoes	shoes	poor people have shoes
2. Nokero			
3. United by Blue			
4. Warby Parker			

F. SYNTHESIZE Discuss the questions in a group.

1. The article discusses a few reasons why the business model has changed. What are these reasons? Do you agree with the author about the reasons for the change? Which reason do you think is the most important?

2. Which person in Reading 2 do you feel the most inspired by? Why?

3. What are some of the qualities that the founders of social businesses have? Do you have any of these qualities? Are there any other qualities that you think are important to be a successful businessperson?

CRITICAL THINKING STRATEGY

Adding details to support statements

When you add **details** to your writing, it helps the reader understand the points or examples you are explaining. One way to add details is to add a follow-up sentence. Look at the chart.

Example	Detail
Hunger is also a problem in the U.S.	It is estimated that 42 million people lack food.
The first bag had a number on it.	That number signified one year of school lunches for one child.

iQ PRACTICE Go online to watch the Critical Thinking Video and check your comprehension. *Practice > Unit 7 > Activity 8*

G. IDENTIFY Read these sentences from Reading 2. In the reading, underline the details that support each sentence. Then choose one of the companies described and go online to find a supporting article about the company.

1. So the company is based on a principle in which it has a product that earns them money, but also allows them to give back to people.

2. Many consumers also like the idea of giving back to the community.

3. Using the one-for-one model, Warby Parker donates a pair of eyeglasses for every pair of Warby Parker eyeglasses purchased.

4. The company tries to solve a global problem, but also is profitable.

5. He started a clothing company, and for each purchase, the company will clean a pound of garbage from "the world's oceans and waterways."

WORK WITH THE VIDEO

A. PREVIEW Do you know what ecotourism is?

VIDEO VOCABULARY

wildlife (n.) animals and plants that live in natural conditions

conservation (n.) the protection of the natural world

alternative (n.) one of two things that you can choose between

vested interest (n. phr.) a strong reason, especially one related to money, for wanting something to happen

iQ RESOURCES Go online to watch the video about ecotourism in Namibia, Africa. *Resources > Video > Unit 7 > Unit Video*

B. CATEGORIZE Watch the video two or three times. Then take notes in the first part of the chart.

	Problems in Namibia	Effects of ecotourism on Namibia
Notes from the video	Tourism depends on seeing wildlife	
My ideas		

C. EXTEND What are some global effects of ecotourism? Write your ideas in the chart above.

WRITE WHAT YOU THINK

SYNTHESIZE Think about Reading 1, Reading 2, and the unit video as you discuss these questions. Then choose one question and write a paragraph in response.

1. After reading about social entrepreneurship, do you think that businesses can be successful and also do good in the world? Why? Why not?

2. Why are social entrepreneurs inspired by seeing their work do good for others? How does this differ from other entrepreneurs?

3. In addition to its main focus, TOMS also provides medical care to people. It has also established factories in poor areas, thus providing jobs. Why do you think social entrepreneurs do additional work like this?

VOCABULARY SKILL Collocations with verbs

Collocations are words that are frequently used together. Learning collocations can improve your vocabulary and can help your writing sound more natural. Look at the examples of collocations with the verbs *provide* and *address*.

> A free school meal provides a way for children to get healthy.
> Solar lamps provide an alternative to kerosene.
> Lauren Bush Lauren's company addresses the issue of child hunger.
> Social entrepreneurs find creative ways to address social problems.

A. IDENTIFY Locate other examples of collocations with the verbs *provide* and *address* in Readings 1 and 2.

B. APPLY Complete the sentences with a form of the verb *address* or *provide*.

1. Many young students hope to _____ climate change.

2. Working from home _____ an alternative for new parents.

3. The organization arranges transportation, and this _____ a way for workers to get to their jobs.

4. Growing sales of the clothing help the company _____ the problem of pollution of oceans.

5. Having a job that paid her a decent wage _____ her with a reason to get up each morning.

iQ PRACTICE Go online for more practice with collocations with verbs.
Practice > Unit 7 > Activity 9

WRITING

OBJECTIVE ▶ At the end of this unit, you will write a cause/effect essay about how a business can do good. This essay will include specific information from the readings, the unit video, and your own ideas.

WRITING SKILL Writing a cause/effect essay

A **cause/effect essay** analyzes the causes (reasons) and effects (results) of a situation or event. A cause/effect essay includes an introductory paragraph, body paragraphs, and a concluding paragraph.

In a cause/effect essay, the introductory paragraph describes the situation or cause, gives background information, and includes a thesis statement (main idea).

The thesis statement in a cause/effect essay describes the effects of the situation.

The body paragraphs of an essay provide support for the thesis statement. In a cause/effect essay, each body paragraph includes a topic sentence that states a supporting point and describes an effect. Other sentences in a body paragraph provide examples, details, or facts.

In a cause/effect essay, the concluding paragraph restates the main idea and often offers some additional thoughts or predictions for the future.

A. WRITING MODEL Read the model cause/effect essay. Underline the thesis statement.

1   When I was in college, I took a class in social economics. We discussed many social problems and brainstormed ways to address them. It was a good way for us to see that we have the power to make changes in the world. I started thinking about social problems in the area where I live. The issue that I saw was the lack of public transportation. I knew of many people who were unable to get to their jobs easily because of the poor public transportation system. Often, they could not afford to have a car. This lack of transportation seemed like a huge problem that I wanted to try to address.

2   I kept thinking about how to find a way to solve this problem. I know many people have cars and don't use them that much. There are also a lot of retired people in my town. I thought maybe I could combine these two groups of people: the ones who had difficulty getting to work and the "seniors" who were retired and had cars sitting in their driveways.

3   I decided to go on social media to find out if there were retired people who might like to help out. The response was amazing! There were many retired men and women who really didn't do that much and were

happy to help drive people to their jobs. I started making lists and maps of where the jobs were, how many people needed transportation, and how many seniors were willing to help. It all started to come together. I matched the drivers with the workers, and both were happy!

4   Now, six months later, I have a carpooling service. I have a steady and growing group of seniors who drive people to work. I have two shifts, one in the morning and one in the evening. (Some seniors prefer not to drive when it's dark.) As of now, the carpool has been successful in getting 25 workers to and from work every day.

5   There has been an additional benefit that I could not have foreseen. The seniors and the workers have become friends. Perhaps their lives would never have crossed if it weren't for this program, but now they help each other out in many ways. For example, one worker is very handy, and he helped a senior fix a broken cabinet in his home. This was an unexpected outcome, and it inspires me to continue with my carpooling project!

B. EXTEND Complete the graphic organizer with information from the essay in Activity A.

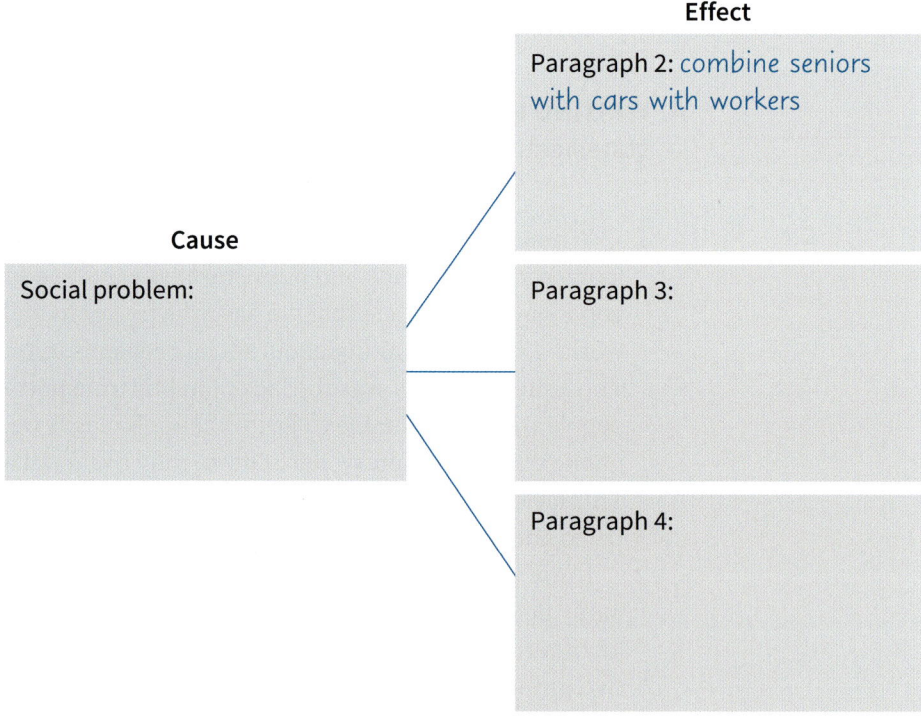

C. WRITING MODEL Read the model cause/effect essay. Then answer the questions on page 180.

1   In 2006, Blake Mycoskie was traveling in South America and noticed that many children there had no shoes. Mycoskie soon found out that shoes are very important to people around the world. Owning a pair of new shoes may not seem like a really big thing to most of us. However, in many poor parts of the world, it *is* a big thing. Owning shoes can have a great impact on people's health, education, and well-being.

2   In many parts of the world, it is fairly common to see people, especially children, walking without shoes. However, there are many dangers to children when they do not wear shoes. In different parts of the world, many diseases, such as hookworm, can be contracted through the feet. Additionally, you can cut your feet on rough terrain or broken glass, which, in some cases, can lead to infection and risk of death. Finally, some climates are quite cold, and lack of footwear can lead to illness. So by simply owning a pair of shoes, a child's health is maintained.

3   A second, and perhaps more important, effect of owning a pair of shoes involves education. In many countries around the world, schools are not free. Parents must pay school fees and provide their children with uniforms, including shoes, in order for them to attend school. In some countries, children are not permitted to go to school if they don't have shoes. An additional benefit to owning a pair of shoes is that a child will be able to go to school.

4   Finally, when children receive new pairs of shoes, it makes them feel better about themselves. In many cases, this may be the first pair of shoes that the child has ever owned. In most cases, it is the first *new* clothing the child has ever owned. In either situation, what this does for a child is improve his or her self-esteem. Children are thrilled to be able to walk through their villages in their new shoes. It makes them feel that they have some worth. An increase in self-esteem is something that is not even measurable.

5   In conclusion, Mycoskie saw a need and established a company that is giving as much as it's getting in profits. So, when you purchase a pair of shoes from this company, you are not only giving to the company but also getting back the satisfaction of knowing that someone else is benefitting in many ways from your purchase.

1. What is the situation or cause that is described in this essay?
   _____

2. Find the thesis statement of the essay. Write it below.
   _____

3. What is the effect or result described in body paragraph 1?
   _____

4. Write one detail or example that the writer used to support the first effect.
   _____

5. What is the effect or result described in body paragraph 2?
   _____

6. Write one detail or example that the writer used to support the second effect.
   _____

7. What is the effect or result described in body paragraph 3?
   _____

8. Write one detail or example that the writer used to support the third effect.
   _____

iQ PRACTICE Go online for more practice with writing a cause/effect essay.
Practice > Unit 7 > Activity 10

Cause and effect: the sun makes plants grow

GRAMMAR Complex sentences

A **complex sentence** has an independent clause, or main clause, and one or more dependent clauses. A clause is a group of words that has a subject and a verb. An independent clause can stand alone as a complete sentence. A dependent clause cannot stand alone and must be used with a main clause. Dependent clauses that show cause can begin with subordinators like *because, since*, and *when*. Look at these examples.

> Lauren Bush Lauren founded the company FEED because she wanted to provide people with a way to help end hunger.
>
> When children are given a nutritious meal, they perform better in school.

The parts of the sentences beginning with *because, since,* and *when* are dependent clauses. If a dependent clause comes before the main clause, it is followed by a comma.

> [dependent clause] Because Bush Lauren had an interest in design, [main clause] she was able to combine this with her desire to help hungry children.

A. IDENTIFY Underline the dependent clauses.

1. Their new computer repair business grew in the first year <u>because they all worked night and day</u>.

2. Since there was very little rain all spring, the amount of corn grown was very small.

3. When he invested $300 in the new company many years ago, he didn't know how much money he would make.

4. The school can now pick up many more children because someone donated another school bus.

5. They were able to finish building the house in a week since many volunteers came to help.

B. APPLY Combine the sentences using the words in parentheses. Add a comma where necessary.

1. Sammy saved all of the money he made in his summer job. He finally had enough money to buy a car. (because)

   <u>Because Sammy saved all of the money he made in his summer job, he finally had enough money to buy a car.</u>

2. The village no longer floods. The villagers planted a hundred trees on the hillside. (since)

3. The organization had received enough donations. It bought the new equipment. (when)

4. Mr. Kelly donated a great deal of money to the children's fund. He knew that the children needed a new school. (because)

5. People in the village suffered from extreme poverty. Many families could not afford to send their children to school. (since)

iQ PRACTICE Go online for more practice with complex sentences.
Practice > Unit 7 > Activities 11–12

UNIT ASSIGNMENT　Write a cause/effect essay

OBJECTIVE ▶

In this assignment, you are going to write a cause/effect essay about how a business can earn money and do good. As you prepare to write, think about the Unit Question, "Can a business earn money while making a difference?" Use information from Reading 1, Reading 2, the unit video, and your work in this unit to support your paragraph. Refer to the Self-Assessment checklist on page 184.

iQ RESOURCES　Go online to the Writing Tutor to read a model cause/effect essay. *Practice > Unit 7 > Activity 13*

PLAN AND WRITE

A. BRAINSTORM　Work in a group. Brainstorm situations in which a business can earn money and still do good. Think of the different companies and people who have done well and done good for society at the same time. What was the problem that they wanted to address? How did they address it?

B. PLAN　Choose one of the situations from Activity A. List at least three effects or results of this situation.

1. _____
2. _____
3. _____

iQ RESOURCES　Go online to download and complete the outline for your cause/effect essay. *Resources > Writing Tools > Unit 7 > Outline*

C. WRITE　Use your planning notes to write your essay.

1. Write your cause/effect essay.
2. Look at the Self-Assessment checklist on page 184 to guide your writing.

iQ PRACTICE　Go online to the Writing Tutor to write your assignment. *Practice > Unit 7 > Activity 14*

REVISE AND EDIT

iQ RESOURCES Go online to download the peer review worksheet.
Resources > Writing Tools > Unit 7 > Peer Review Worksheet

A. PEER REVIEW Read your partner's essay. Then use the peer review worksheet (*Resource > Unit 7 > Pear Review*). Discuss the review with your partner.

B. REWRITE Based on your partner's review, revise and rewrite your essay.

C. EDIT Complete the Self-Assessment checklist as you prepare to write the final draft of your essay. Be prepared to hand in your work or discuss it in class.

SELF-ASSESSMENT	Yes	No
Does the Introductory paragraph contain a thesis statement?	☐	☐
Does the introductory paragraph describe the situation (cause) and its effects?	☐	☐
Does the essay include three body paragraphs that each describe an effect?	☐	☐
Does the essay include a concluding paragraph that summarizes the situation (cause) and its effects?	☐	☐
Does the essay include complex sentences? If not, where could one or two be added?	☐	☐
Does the essay include collocations with verbs? If not, where could one or two be added?	☐	☐
Does the essay include vocabulary from the unit?	☐	☐
Did you check the essay for punctuation, spelling, and grammar?	☐	☐

D. REFLECT Discuss these questions with a partner or group.

1. What is something new you learned in this unit?
2. Look back at the Unit Question—Can a business earn money while making a difference? Is your answer different now than it was when you started the unit? If yes, how is it different? Why?

iQ PRACTICE Go to the online discussion board to discuss the questions.
Practice > Unit 7 > Activity 15

TRACK YOUR SUCCESS

iQ PRACTICE Go to the online to check the words and phrases you have learned in the unit. *Practice › Unit 7 › Activity 16*

Check (✓) the skills and strategies you learned. If you need more work on a skill, refer to the page(s) in parentheses.

READING	☐ I can use a timeline. (p. 165)
CRITICAL THINKING	☐ I can add details to my writing to support a statement. (p. 174)
VOCABULARY	☐ I can use collocations with verbs. (p. 176)
WRITING	☐ I can write a cause/effect essay. (p. 177)
GRAMMAR	☐ I can use complex sentences. (p. 181)
OBJECTIVE ▶	☐ I can gather information and ideas to write a cause/effect essay about how a business can earn money and do good.

Behavioral Studies

8

READING scanning a text
CRITICAL THINKING identifying problems and solutions
VOCABULARY collocations with adjectives + prepositions
WRITING writing an argumentative essay
GRAMMAR sentence fragments

UNIT QUESTION

What does it take to be successful?

A. Discuss these questions with your classmates.

1. How does someone become a successful athlete?
2. What are some things people give up or sacrifice in order to be successful?
3. Look at the photo. What do you think these women needed to do in order to be successful?

B. Listen to *The Q Classroom* online. Then answer these questions.

1. Felix believes success does not have to be about money or a career. How can a person be successful without earning a lot of money?
2. Sophy believes that people can't be successful by themselves. Do you agree or disagree? Why?
3. Marcus states that people need to be able to adapt to changes in order to be successful. Do you feel the same way? Can you give an example?

iQ PRACTICE Go to the online discussion board to discuss the Unit Question with your classmates. *Practice > Unit 8 > Activity 1*

UNIT OBJECTIVE ▶ Read the articles and gather information and ideas to write an argumentative essay about what it takes to be successful.

READING

READING 1

OBJECTIVE ▶

Fast Cars, Big Money

You are going to read an article from a business magazine about the popular sport of car racing, written from a business perspective. Use the article to gather information and ideas for your Unit Assignment.

PREVIEW THE READING

A. PREVIEW Read the headings. What do you think is the purpose of the article? Check (✓) your answer.

- ☐ to explain the sport of Formula 1 car racing
- ☐ to encourage businesses to invest in car racing
- ☐ to compare Formula 1 car races around the world
- ☐ to show why car racing is an expensive sport

B. QUICK WRITE What are some ways businesses attract more customers? Write for 5–10 minutes in response. Be sure to use this section for your Unit Assignment.

C. VOCABULARY Check (✓) the words you know. Then work with a partner to locate each word in the reading. Use clues to help define the words you don't know. Check your definitions in the dictionary.

assured *(adj.)*	invest *(v.)* 🗝	profit *(n.)* 🗝
dependable *(adj.)*	logo *(n.)*	sponsor *(v.)* 🗝
expansion *(n.)* OPAL	market *(n.)* 🗝	stability *(n.)* OPAL
image *(n.)* 🗝 OPAL		

🗝 Oxford 3000™ words   OPAL Oxford Phrasal Academic Lexicon

iQ PRACTICE Go online to listen and practice your pronunciation.
Practice > Unit 8 > Activity 2

188   UNIT 8   What does it take to be successful?

WORK WITH THE READING

A. INVESTIGATE Read the article and gather information about what it takes to be successful.

FAST CARS, BIG MONEY

DOES YOUR BUSINESS NEED A BOOST?

1   Imagine 350 million people seeing your company **logo** every year. Imagine this number growing even higher every year. Imagine being part of one of the most prestigious[1] and glamorous[2] sports in the world and making millions of dollars at the same time. Sound attractive? Hundreds of companies have already discovered the financial benefits of **sponsoring** Formula 1 racing. When you choose to sponsor a team, you can be **assured** that your company will grow financially and globally.

WHY ARE COMPANIES INTERESTED?

2   Companies have realized that investments in the sport of auto racing can bring them huge **profits**. Businesses, including banks, hotels, and telecommunication companies, **invest** tens of millions of dollars every year to sponsor race teams. Hundreds of millions of people watch car races every year. For companies, this is an enormous **market**.

3   Cars race around the track with company logos stuck to the doors, hood, and trunk, and people notice. Corporate sponsors can invest $5 million in a race team and make $30 million or more from car advertising. These costs are cheap compared to the profits. Sponsoring a team also shows the financial **stability** of your company. Race cars can cost tens of millions of dollars, and race teams can spend up to $300 million a year. Companies who invest in race teams are showing the world that they are powerful and **dependable**.

WHY IS INVESTING NOW A GOOD IDEA?

4   Much of Formula 1's current success comes from its **expansion** to global markets. Although most races are in Europe, today there are races in the Middle East and Asia. Companies support worldwide expansion because it gives them new customers in emerging markets. They can push their brand[3] globally. Many companies have already invested in Formula 1's most recent host locations, including Bahrain, Abu Dhabi, and Singapore. As a result, they have been able to expand their business to the Middle East and

Formula 1 race car

---

[1] **prestigious:** respected or admired because of success
[2] **glamorous:** attractive or full of glamor
[3] **brand:** the name of a product that is made by a particular company

Asia. These areas of the world are full of business opportunities, and Formula 1 racing has brought them more growth and success. Expanding overseas also shows that your company has a global message, which is important in today's global economy.

WHY SHOULD MY COMPANY INVEST?

5   Thanks to a strong business mentality, Formula 1 racing has become a profitable sport for corporations to invest in. The global economy is always changing, but the industry has succeeded by finding new ways to make more money. Sponsoring a team will not only bring your company profits, but will also improve your company's **image** as a business that is stable and globally-minded. Take advantage of this wonderful business opportunity and enjoy being part of this glamorous, thrill-seeking[4] sport. Vroom vroom!

[4] **thrill-seeking:** trying to find pleasure in excitement

B. VOCABULARY Here are some words from Reading 1. Read the sentences. Circle the word or phrase that can replace the bold word without changing the meaning of the sentence.

1. A company **logo** often gives the full name of the company or the first letter of the name. *(symbol)* / *address* / *rule*

2. Many companies regularly **sponsor** sports teams so that they can put advertising on their uniforms. *support* / *watch* / *buy*

3. A brand-new business cannot be **assured** that it will succeed right away. *worried* / *sure* / *interested*

4. Businesses need to make a **profit** consistently in order to be successful. *income* / *friends* / *decisions*

5. When companies **invest** money to make a new product, they have to consider the costs carefully. *need* / *lose* / *spend*

6. The Internet has given businesses access to a bigger **market** around the world. *number of customers* / *number of difficulties* / *number of computers*

7. Large companies generally have more **stability** than small businesses. *choice* / *strength* / *problems*

8. It is wise to invest in **dependable** companies because they tend to manage their money well. *new* / *reliable* / *different*

9. There has been a large **expansion** in the number of bilingual jobs because of the global economy. *decrease* / *growth* / *cost*

10. In order to be successful, a business needs to consider its **image**, or the way the public sees it. *attitude* / *appearance* / *growth*

iQ PRACTICE Go online for more practice with the vocabulary.
Practice › Unit 8 › Activity 3

C. IDENTIFY Read the main ideas. Write the paragraph number where they are found.

____ 1. By sponsoring a Formula 1 team, a company will grow financially and globally.

____ 2. Formula 1 sponsorship is profitable and shows that a company is powerful and reliable.

____ 3. Sponsors can make a lot of money from car advertising.

____ 4. Formula 1 racing is a good investment today because of its expansion to global markets.

____ 5. Sponsorship brings companies profits and improves their image.

WRITING TIP

Activity E asks you to write a summary using the graphic organizer in Activity D. Use a graphic organizer before you write a summary to help you see how the ideas in a text are organized.

D. CATEGORIZE Work with a partner or group. Complete the graphic organizer for Reading 1. List two reasons that answer each question.

	Reason 1	Reason 2
1. Why are companies interested in Formula 1 racing?	Companies can make huge profits.	
2. Why is investing in Formula 1 racing now a good idea?		It shows that a company has a global message.
3. Why should companies invest in Formula 1 racing?		

E. COMPOSE Write a summary of Reading 1. Use the graphic organizer in Activity D to help you write your summary.

WRITING TIP

Activity F asks you to identify what the words *this* and *these* refer to in a previous sentence. Writers use *this* and *these* to continue an idea in a following sentence. Use *this* for a singular noun. Use *these* for a plural noun.

F. IDENTIFY Read these sentences from Reading 1. Then answer the questions. Find the sentences in the reading to help you.

1. (Paragraph 1) Imagine **this** number growing even higher every year.

   What number does *this* refer to? _____

2. (Paragraph 2) For companies, **this** is an enormous market.

   What market does *this* refer to? _____

3. (Paragraph 3) **This** cost is cheap compared to the profits.

   What costs does *this* refer to? _____

4. (Paragraph 4) **These** areas of the world are full of business opportunities.

   What areas of the world does **these** refer to? _____

5. (Paragraph 5) Take advantage of **this** wonderful business opportunity and enjoy being part of **this** glamorous, thrill-seeking sport.

   a. What business opportunity does **this** refer to? _____

   b. What sport does **this** refer to? _____

iQ PRACTICE Go online for additional reading and comprehension.
Practice > Unit 8 > Activity 4

WRITE WHAT YOU THINK

A. DISCUSS Discuss the questions in a group.

1. Is sponsoring Formula 1 racing a good or bad investment? Explain.

2. Do you think that businesses that sponsor sports like car racing would be as successful without giving sponsorship money? Why or why not?

3. Why do you think banks choose to advertise on Formula 1 racing cars?

B. COMPOSE Choose one of the questions from Activity A and write a paragraph in response. Look back at your Quick Write on page 188 as you think about what you learned.

READING SKILL Scanning a text

Scanning means looking through a text quickly to find specific information, such as names, numbers, and dates. We scan items like the newspaper, a timetable, a dictionary, and the table of contents in a book. When you scan, do not read every word. Look for key words or phrases that will help you find the answer quickly. Think about how the information will appear on the page. For example, if you are looking for a date, scan only for numbers.

A. APPLY Scan Reading 1 for the missing information. Use key words in the sentences to help you find the answers. Then complete each statement.

1. Businesses that sponsor race teams include _____, _____, and _____.

2. Company logos are stuck to the _____, _____, and _____ of race cars.

3. Although most Formula 1 races are in Europe, today there are races in _____ and _____.

B. IDENTIFY Scan Reading 1 again for the missing numbers. Use key words in the sentences to help you find the answers. Then complete each statement.

1. Every year, _____ million people watch Formula 1 races.

2. Businesses invest _____ of _____ of dollars every year to sponsor race teams.

3. Corporate sponsors can invest just _____ in a race team and make _____ or more.

4. Race teams can spend up to _____ a year.

iQ PRACTICE Go online for more practice with scanning a text.
Practice > Unit 8 > Activity 5

READING 2

Practice Makes . . . Pain?

OBJECTIVE ▶

You are going to read a newspaper article about child athletes and what they do to succeed in sports. Use the article to gather information and ideas for your Unit Assignment.

PREVIEW THE READING

A. PREVIEW Look at the title. What do you think the writer will say about child athletes? Check (✓) your answer.

☐ It's easy for children to be successful in sports if they start early.

☐ The sacrifices children make for success in sports are sometimes too great.

WRITING TIP
Remember to use reasons to explain the main idea in your topic sentence.

B. QUICK WRITE Are competitive sports good for children? Write for 5–10 minutes in response. Include a topic sentence and supporting details. Be sure to use this section for your Unit Assignment.

C. VOCABULARY Check (✓) the words you know. Then work with a partner to locate each word in the reading.

aggressively *(adv.)*	due to *(prep. phr.)* OPAL	recover *(v.)* 🔑
dedication *(n.)*	exception *(n.)* OPAL	sign *(n.)* 🔑
demanding *(adj.)*	motion *(n.)*	trend *(n.)* 🔑 OPAL

🔑 Oxford 3000™ words   OPAL Oxford Phrasal Academic Lexicon

iQ PRACTICE Go online to listen and practice your pronunciation.
Practice > Unit 8 > Activity 6

WORK WITH THE READING

 A. INVESTIGATE Read the article and gather information about what it takes to be successful.

PRACTICE MAKES ... PAIN

1   At ten, Courtney Thompson was a top-ranked gymnast in New Hampshire. She had been doing flips since she was one and had her heart set on competing in the Olympics. She practiced four and a half hours a day, six days a week, often repeating the same move 100 times. Her **demanding** schedule took a toll[1]. It got to the point where Courtney could barely straighten her elbows unless she put ice on them. On January 12, 2005, she had to stop in the middle of a floor routine. "I jumped up and grabbed my arm. It hurt really bad."

2   Doctors discovered that Courtney's constant workouts had caused the cartilage, or connective tissue, in her elbow to separate from the bone. She had surgery on both arms and went through months of painful rehabilitation[2]. Courtney's experience is part of a growing **trend** in youth sports—kids and teens were starting to have the same type of injuries that only professional athletes used to have. Experts say kids are pushing their bodies to the limit, practicing sports too hard for too long. The exhausting schedules often lead to dangerous injuries that could keep young athletes from competing—permanently.

⊙ Under Strain

3   According to experts at *The Physician and Sportsmedicine* journal, between 30 and 50 percent of youth sports injuries are **due to** overuse. Overuse injuries are caused by repetitive **motion** that, over time, puts more stress on a body part than it can handle. The tissue or bone eventually breaks, stretches, or tears.

4   Danny Clark ended up with an overuse injury last year. The teen baseball player from Altamonte Springs, Florida, hurt himself by throwing 80 pitches in a single game after two months of not pitching at all. The sudden repetitive action tore Danny's rotator cuff. The rotator cuff is a group of four muscles and the tendons that connect them to bones in the shoulder. Afterward, he couldn't pitch

---

[1] **take a toll:** to have a negative effect
[2] **rehabilitation:** the process of returning to a normal life again after an injury

UNIT 5

bravely *(adv.)* B1
conquer *(v.)* C1
determined *(adj.)* OPAL B1
distinctive *(adj.)* OPAL C1
earn *(v.)* A2
element *(n.)* OPAL B1
emerge *(v.)* OPAL B2
enable *(v.)* OPAL B2
goal *(n.)* OPAL A2
perceive *(v.)* OPAL B2
poverty *(n.)* OPAL B1
predict *(v.)* OPAL A2
role *(n.)* OPAL A2
set apart *(v. phr.)* C2
significant *(adj.)* OPAL B2
threat *(n.)* OPAL B2
trait *(n.)* B2
traumatic *(adj.)* C1
ultimate *(adj.)* OPAL B2

UNIT 6

according to *(prep.)* OPAL A2
arrogant *(adj.)* B2
come up with *(v. phr.)* B1
complex *(adj.)* OPAL B2
deal with *(v. phr.)* A2
efficient *(adj.)* OPAL B1
experiment *(n.)* OPAL A2
function *(v.)* OPAL B2
have a gift *(v. phr.)* B2
impatient *(adj.)* B2
make sense *(v. phr.)* A2
move on *(v. phr.)* C1
pace *(n.)* B2
proof *(n.)* B2
rely on *(v. phr.)* B2
revolutionary *(adj.)* C1
subject *(n.)* OPAL C1
view *(v.)* OPAL B1

UNIT 7

address *(v.)* OPAL B2
aspect *(n.)* OPAL B2
concerned *(adj.)* OPAL B2
desire *(n.)* OPAL B2
distribute *(v.)* OPAL B2
estimate *(v.)* OPAL B2
firsthand *(adv.)* C1
focus *(n.)* OPAL A2
give back *(v. phr.)* B1
inspired *(adj.)* B2
massive *(adj.)* B2
model *(n.)* OPAL A2
movement *(n.)* OPAL C1
opportunity *(n.)* OPAL B1
overall *(adj.)* OPAL B2
prospect *(n.)* B2
reusable *(adj.)* C1
seek *(v.)* OPAL B2
signify *(v.)* C1

UNIT 8

aggressively *(adv.)* B2
assured *(adj.)* C2
dedication *(n.)* C1
demanding *(adj.)* B2
dependable *(adj.)* C1
due to *(prep. phr.)* OPAL B1
exception *(n.)* OPAL B2
expansion *(n.)* OPAL B2
image *(n.)* OPAL A2
invest *(v.)* B1
logo *(n.)* B2
market *(n.)* B1
motion *(n.)* B2
profit *(n.)* B1
recover *(v.)* B2
sign *(n.)* A2
sponsor *(v.)* B2
stability *(n.)* OPAL C1
trend *(n.)* OPAL B1

VOCABULARY LIST AND CEFR CORRELATION

🔑 The **Oxford 3000**™ is a list of the 3,000 core words that every learner of English needs to know. The words have been chosen based on their frequency in the Oxford English Corpus and relevance to learners of English. Every word is aligned to the CEFR, guiding learners on the words they should know at the A1–B2 level.

OPAL The **Oxford Phrasal Academic Lexicon** is an essential guide to the most important words and phrases to know for academic English. The word lists are based on the Oxford Corpus of Academic English and the British Academic Spoken English corpus.

The **Common European Framework of Reference for Language (CEFR)** provides a basic description of what language learners have to do to use language effectively. The system contains 6 reference levels: A1, A2, B1, B2, C1, C2.

UNIT 1

accomplishment *(n.)* C1
authentic *(adj.)* C1
appreciate *(v.)* 🔑 B1
consider *(v.)* 🔑 OPAL A2
confidence *(n.)* 🔑 B2
demonstrate *(v.)* 🔑 OPAL B2
effective *(adj.)* 🔑 OPAL B1
expect *(v.)* 🔑 OPAL A2
impress *(v.)* 🔑 B2
lead to *(v. phr.)* A2
maintain *(v.)* 🔑 OPAL B2
offensive *(adj.)* 🔑 B2
professional *(adj.)* 🔑 OPAL A2
punctual *(adj.)* C1
research *(n.)* 🔑 OPAL A2
responsible *(adj.)* 🔑 OPAL B1
select *(v.)* 🔑 OPAL B2
slang *(n.)* B2
stranger *(n.)* 🔑 B1
weakness *(n.)* 🔑 B2

UNIT 2

arrange *(v.)* 🔑 B2
artistic *(adj.)* 🔑 B2
at risk *(prep. phr.)* B1
balanced *(adj.)* OPAL B2
be made up of *(v. phr.)* B2
be willing to *(v. phr.)* B1
identical *(adj.)* OPAL B2
identify *(v.)* 🔑 OPAL B2
influence *(v.)* 🔑 OPAL B2
in terms of *(prep. phr.)* OPAL B1
likely *(adj.)* 🔑 OPAL B1
method *(n.)* 🔑 OPAL B1
occasion *(n.)* 🔑 B1
principle *(n.)* 🔑 OPAL B2
recognize *(v.)* 🔑 OPAL B1
sensitive *(adj.)* 🔑 OPAL B2
status symbol *(n.)* C1
system *(n.)* 🔑 OPAL A2
typically *(adv.)* 🔑 OPAL B1

UNIT 3

adapt *(v.)* 🔑 OPAL B2
data *(n.)* 🔑 OPAL A2
digital *(adj.)* 🔑 OPAL A2
discover *(v.)* 🔑 B1
feedback *(n.)* 🔑 B2
global *(adj.)* 🔑 OPAL B2
in favor of *(prep. phr.)* B1
interactive *(adj.)* OPAL C1
limitation *(n.)* OPAL B2
manufacturer *(n.)* B2
monitor *(v.)* 🔑 OPAL C1
obey *(v.)* 🔑 B2
obstacle *(n.)* B2
occur *(v.)* 🔑 OPAL B2
reliable *(adj.)* 🔑 OPAL B1
respond *(v.)* 🔑 OPAL B2
revolutionize *(v.)* C1
sense *(v.)* 🔑 OPAL B2
the benefits of *(n. phr.)* OPAL A2

UNIT 4

accurate *(adj.)* 🔑 OPAL B1
acknowledge *(v.)* 🔑 OPAL B2
annoying *(adj.)* 🔑 B1
annual *(adj.)* 🔑 OPAL B2
broadcasting *(n.)* B2
donation *(n.)* B2
entertain *(v.)* 🔑 B1
exposure *(n.)* C1
factor *(n.)* 🔑 OPAL A2
impact *(n.)* 🔑 OPAL B1
imply *(v.)* 🔑 OPAL B2
memorable *(adj.)* B2
reflect *(v.)* 🔑 OPAL B2
relevant *(adj.)* 🔑 OPAL B2
specifically *(adv.)* 🔑 OPAL B1
suggest *(v.)* 🔑 OPAL B2
support *(v.)* 🔑 OPAL B1
surrounding *(adj.)* 🔑 B2

TRACK YOUR SUCCESS

iQ PRACTICE Go online to check the words and phrases you have learned in this unit. *Practice > Unit 8 > Activity 16*

Check (✓) the skills you learned. If you need more work on a skill, refer to the page(s) in parentheses.

READING	☐ I can scan a text. (p. 192)
CRITICAL THINKING	☐ I can identify problems and solutions. (p. 197)
VOCABULARY	☐ I can use collocations with adjectives + prepositions. (p. 200)
WRITING	☐ I can write an argumentative essay (p. 202)
GRAMMAR	☐ I can recognize and avoid sentence fragments. (p. 206)
OBJECTIVE ▶	☐ I can gather information and ideas to write an argumentative essay about what it takes to be successful.

REVISE AND EDIT

iQ RESOURCES Go online to download the peer review worksheet.
Resources > Writing Tools > Unit 8 > Peer Review Worksheet

A. PEER REVIEW Read your partner's essay. Then use the peer review worksheet. Discuss the review with your partner.

B. REWRITE Based on your partner's review, revise and rewrite your essay.

C. EDIT Complete the Self-Assessment checklist as you prepare to write the final draft of your essay. Be prepared to hand in your work or discuss it in class.

SELF-ASSESSMENT	Yes	No
Does the essay include an introductory paragraph that states an opinion and describes a counterargument?	☐	☐
Does the essay include three body paragraphs that each provide a reason and supporting examples or facts?	☐	☐
Does the essay contain a concluding paragraph that restates the opinion, refers to the counterargument, and summarizes the reasons?	☐	☐
Are there any sentence fragments? Underline them and then correct them.	☐	☐
Are adjective + preposition collocations used correctly?	☐	☐
Does the essay include vocabulary from the unit?	☐	☐
Did you check the essay for punctuation, spelling, and grammar?	☐	☐

D. REFLECT Discuss these questions with a partner or group.

1. What is something new you learned in this unit?
2. Look back at the Unit Question—What does it take to be successful? Is your answer different now than when you started the unit? If yes, how is it different? Why?

iQ PRACTICE Go to the online discussion board to discuss the questions.
Practice > Unit 8 > Activity 15

PLAN AND WRITE

A. BRAINSTORM Follow these steps to help you organize your ideas.

1. Choose your topic from the box. Then look at the list of sports. Check (✓) the sport(s) you would like to discuss in your essay.

   > Should athletes or sports teams accept money from corporate sponsors in order to be successful? Discuss one or more specific sports in your essay.
   >
   > Should child athletes be pushed hard in order to succeed? Discuss one or more specific sports in your essay.

   ☐ American football   ☐ rugby
   ☐ baseball   ☐ running
   ☐ basketball   ☐ soccer
   ☐ Formula 1 racing   ☐ tennis
   ☐ gymnastics   ☐ (other) _____

2. Brainstorm reasons that will help support your opinion about the topic.

3. Brainstorm a counterargument for your essay. Why would someone disagree with your opinion?

B. PLAN Follow these steps to plan your essay.

1. Write a thesis statement for your essay that expresses your opinion about the topic. List your three best reasons from Activity A.

   _____
   _____
   _____

2. Think about the readings and the unit video in this unit. Is there any information that can help support your ideas?

iQ RESOURCES Go online to download and complete the outline for your argumentative essay. *Resources > Writing Tools > Unit 8 > Outline*

C. WRITE Use your planning notes to write your essay.

1. Write your argumentative essay that explains what it takes to be successful. Be sure to use reasons and examples or facts to support your thesis statement.

2. Look at the Self-Assessment checklist on page 209 to guide your writing.

iQ PRACTICE Go online to the Writing Tutor to write your assignment. *Practice > Unit 8 > Activity 14*

A. CATEGORIZE Identify each sentence as a complete sentence (*S*) or a sentence fragment (*F*). Correct the sentence fragments with a partner.

____ 1. When athletes feel pain.

____ 2. She always stretches for 20 minutes before she exercises.

____ 3. Because there are more children in competitive sports.

____ 4. Since I started playing soccer, I have lost weight.

____ 5. Although baseball looks easy to play.

B. APPLY Read the paragraph and correct any fragments.

   I loved playing basketball in high school because it helped me make a lot of new friends. When I was young. I was a very shy person. It was difficult for me to speak with people. Because I was so shy. Then a classmate invited me to try out for the basketball team. I was pretty good, and I was picked for the team. Although I was nervous at first. I really enjoyed working with my teammates. We were like a family. We supported each other. When we played together against other schools. Many of us became good friends off the court, too. Little by little, I learned not to be so shy. Today I still keep in touch with my old teammates on social networking sites. Although we don't see each other anymore. We are still good friends. Thanks to them, I'm not shy like I used to be back in high school.

iQ PRACTICE Go online for more practice with sentence fragments. *Practice > Unit 8 > Activities 11–12*

UNIT ASSIGNMENT   Write an argumentative essay
OBJECTIVE ▶

In this assignment, you are going to write an argumentative essay about what it takes to be successful. As you prepare your essay, think about the Unit Question, "What does it take to be successful?" Use information from Reading 1, Reading 2, the unit video, and your work in this unit to support your essay. Refer to the Self-Assessment checklist on page 209.

iQ PRACTICE Go online to the Writing Tutor to read a model argumentative essay. *Practice > Unit 8 > Activity 13*

However, they also have to think about the consequences. I think parents will regret their decision later on because they will have missed out on important days and events in their children's lives, as well as moments when their children really needed them by their side. In addition, parents could be wasting their money, since only a small number of athletes make it to the Olympics, even if they show a lot of potential at a young age. For these three reasons, parents need to think very hard before making a decision that could negatively affect their lives and their children's lives for years to come.

2. Which sentence restates the writer's opinion and summarizes the first two reasons? Underline it.

3. According to the conclusion, what was the topic of the third body paragraph?
   _____
   _____

4. What prediction does the writer make at the end of the conclusion?
   _____
   _____

5. Do you agree or disagree with the writer's prediction? Why? Share your answer with a partner.

iQ PRACTICE Go online for more practice with writing an argumentative essay. *Practice > Unit 8 > Activity 10*

GRAMMAR Sentence fragments

A **sentence fragment** is an incomplete sentence that cannot stand alone. Sentence fragments are usually considered errors. It is important to avoid sentence fragments in your writing. Look at the examples.

Fragment: When children play soccer.
Fragment: Because children can get injured.

As you learned in Unit 7, these examples are **dependent clauses**. When used alone, they are fragments. They need to be combined with a main clause.

<u>When children play soccer</u>, they learn the importance of teamwork.
Parents worry about competitive sports <u>because children can get injured</u>.

Words such as *because*, *since*, *although*, *when*, or *after* are often used with dependent clauses. These words connect an incomplete sentence to a main clause to avoid a fragment.

together every night or go shopping together whenever they want. Parents could also miss out on important events, like birthdays or the first day at a new school. I think parents will regret their decision when their children are grown up and they have missed these important days and events.

1. Circle the sentence in the introductory paragraph that states the counterargument.

2. Underline the sentence in the introductory paragraph that gives the writer's opinion about the topic.

3. What reason does the writer give to support his or her opinion? Circle the sentence in the body paragraph that states the reason.

4. The writer states, "Sending children away may make them better athletes, but it cannot replace **this lost time** together." What does this lost time refer to?

   _____

5. What examples does the writer use to support his or her reason in the body paragraph?

   Example 1: _not able to read together every night_

   Example 2: _____

   Example 3: _____

   Example 4: _____

6. Do you think the writer's first reason is convincing? Why or why not? Share your answer with a partner.

WRITING TIP
Activity D asks you to provide examples. Writers often use *for example* and *for instance* to signal examples. *For example* and *for instance* usually begin a new sentence and are followed by a comma.

D. COMPOSE Read the topic sentence for a second body paragraph for the essay assignment in Activity C. Write 5–8 supporting sentences for the paragraph. Include examples to support the reason in the topic sentence.

   Second, parents who send their children to train far away from home will not be able to be around when their children need them. For example,

E. EVALUATE Read this concluding paragraph for the essay assignment in Activity C. Then answer the questions.

1. Which sentence refers to the counterargument? Circle it.

   Many parents think letting their child athlete train far away from home is a good idea because it will help them compete in the Olympics one day.

Reason 2: _____

_____

Reason 3: _____

_____

3. Look at the concluding paragraph. Which sentence refers to the counterargument? Circle it. Which sentence restates the writer's opinion? Underline it.

4. What additional idea does the writer include in the concluding paragraph? Why do you think the writer added this idea?

_____

_____

TIP FOR SUCCESS

Activity B asks you to give your opinion about something you've read. When you state whether you agree or disagree with an author, include reasons for your opinion so that your ideas are well supported.

B. COMPOSE Look again at the model essay in Activity A. Do you agree or disagree with the writer? Write a paragraph of 5–8 sentences giving your opinion. Include reasons to support your opinion.

C. WRITING MODEL Read the essay question. Then read the introductory paragraph and first body paragraph of the model argumentative essay. Answer the questions on page 205.

Essay question: *Should parents let their child athletes leave home at an early age so they can train for the Olympics?*

Experts agree that child athletes are training harder and longer than they did in the past. Compared to before, children today who take up competitive sports, like figure skating or gymnastics, train so seriously that many leave home at a young age to follow their dream. In fact, gymnasts as young as eight years old may leave home and live far away to train with the best coaches. This is because many parents believe good coaches will give their children the opportunity to compete in the Olympics one day, and it is worth the sacrifice. However, I believe sending athletes away from home so young is not the right choice. Parents of these young competitive athletes should not let them leave home to train for the Olympics for three important reasons.

First of all, parents should not let their children leave home to train because they lose precious time with them. Children will not live with their parents forever. The years they spend with their parents go very quickly. One day they're in kindergarten, and the next day it seems like they're off to college. Sending children away may make them better athletes, but it cannot replace this lost time together. For example, they won't be able to read

First, playing competitive soccer keeps children in good shape. Soccer players build strength, flexibility, and endurance. Unlike some sports, soccer requires children to move around constantly. This constant motion helps players build muscles and burn fat more efficiently. Running not only strengthens leg muscles, but also burns a lot of calories, and it improves heart health. Children who play less active competitive sports, like baseball, do not enjoy these same advantages because they can spend long stretches of time just standing around.

Second, being a competitive soccer player teaches children the importance of teamwork. A soccer team has 11 players and several positions. Forwards score goals, fullbacks and goalies defend, and halfbacks assist both forwards and fullbacks. All of these players depend on each other during a game. Therefore, they have to learn to communicate well, and they must trust one another if they want to win. Learning teamwork, good communication skills, and trust will not just help children succeed on a competitive soccer team. The truth is these skills and values will also be useful in their lives at home, at school, and eventually, into adulthood.

Finally, competitive soccer is one of the best ways for children to learn about discipline. Players often practice after school or early in the morning, and they have games on the weekend. Young soccer players, however, also have to worry about completing all their schoolwork. In order to do both successfully, children learn how to manage their time effectively to meet homework deadlines and to show up to soccer practice on time. Competitive players also have to take good care of themselves by eating healthy food and keeping their bodies in good shape, which teaches them self-control.

There are still parents out there who will not put their children in competitive soccer because of the risk of injury. However, I believe this wonderful sport actually has many advantages over other sports. These children are often in excellent shape, and most importantly, they are learning values and skills that they will carry with them into adulthood, like discipline and teamwork. As long as parents monitor their children, they can help to make sure they avoid possible injury, and in that case, everybody wins.

1. Look at the introductory paragraph. What is the counterargument? Circle it. Which sentence states the writer's opinion about the topic? Underline it.

2. Look at the body paragraphs. What are the three reasons that the writer gives for his or her opinion?

   Reason 1: _____

   _____

WRITING

OBJECTIVE ▶ At the end of this unit, you will write an argumentative essay about what it takes to be successful. This essay will include specific information from the readings, the unit video, and your own ideas.

WRITING SKILL Writing an argumentative essay

An **argumentative essay** expresses how the writer feels about a topic. For example, it might express whether the writer agrees or disagrees with an idea.

The introductory paragraph in an argumentative essay includes the thesis statement, which clearly states the writer's opinion or view about a topic. The introductory paragraph may include background information and a **counterargument** to the writer's opinion. A counterargument is the opposite opinion. Writers sometimes mention a counterargument and then explain why it's not true in order to make their point stronger.

Each body paragraph of an argumentative essay includes a topic sentence that states a reason for the writer's opinion. Examples or facts are given to support each reason.

The concluding paragraph of an argumentative essay restates the opinion and refers to the counterargument. The concluding paragraph also summarizes the reasons the writer has this opinion. Often, the concluding paragraph includes an additional idea, sometimes a prediction, about the topic.

TIP FOR SUCCESS
Writers use certain phrases to introduce a counterargument, such as *some people say that, some people think that,* and *some people argue that.*

A. WRITING MODEL Read the model argumentative essay. Then answer the questions on pages 203–204.

Competitive Soccer: An Ideal Sport for Children

Soccer is the most popular sport in the world, and for many people, it is an important part of their childhood. Many children join competitive soccer leagues at a very young age. Some parents, however, believe that competitive soccer is too dangerous. They worry about their children getting a serious injury, so they decide to put them in a less aggressive team sport like basketball or baseball. I don't think this is a good enough reason not to let children play soccer. The fact is that children can get injured playing any sport. Even baseball players can get serious injuries. If children aren't allowed to join competitive soccer leagues, I believe they will miss out on very important advantages of playing this wonderful sport. Soccer is an ideal sport for children, and as a competitive soccer player, a child will not only get a good physical workout, but will also learn valuable lessons about teamwork and discipline.

7. Are you _____ going to the baseball game tonight? I have an extra ticket if you'd like to go.

8. The gymnast was _____ competing for the first time in front of hundreds of people.

B. COMPOSE Choose five adjective + preposition collocations from Activity A. Write a sentence using each collocation.

1. _____
   _____
2. _____
   _____
3. _____
   _____
4. _____
   _____
5. _____
   _____

iQ PRACTICE Go online for more practice with using collocations with adjectives + prepositions. *Practice > Unit 8 > Activity 9*

WRITE WHAT YOU THINK

SYNTHESIZE Think about Reading 1, Reading 2, and the unit video as you discuss these questions. Then choose one question and write a paragraph in response.

1. What are some ways that athletes pay for success?
2. How do parents of child athletes pay for success? Consider financial, physical, and psychological costs in your response.

VOCABULARY SKILL Collocations with adjectives + prepositions

Collocations are words that frequently go together. One common pattern for collocations is adjective + preposition.

Adjective + Preposition		Adjective + Preposition	
interested	in	famous	for
due	to	upset	about

Learning collocations will help you increase your vocabulary and improve your writing.

iQ RESOURCES Go online to watch the Vocabulary Skill Video.
Resources > Video > Unit 8 > Vocabulary Skill Video

ACADEMIC LANGUAGE

The corpus shows that *due to* is more common in academic writing than academic speaking.

OPAL
Oxford Phrasal Academic Lexicon

A. APPLY Complete the sentences with the adjective + preposition collocations from the box.

~~afraid of~~	famous for	involved in	sure about
due to	interested in	nervous about	upset about

1. Parents whose children compete in sports are often _afraid of_ injuries.
2. The player's injury was _____ overuse.
3. Carlos was not _____ about the rules of the game, so he asked his coach.
4. Felix was very _____ losing the championship game. He really wanted to win.
5. Nadia Comăneci is _____ being one of the greatest gymnasts in history.
6. More children are _____ organized sports at a very young age today. My neighbor's son started playing soccer when he was four.

WORK WITH THE VIDEO

A. PREVIEW Should universities give athletes money so that they can attend college? Share your opinion with a partner.

VIDEO VOCABULARY

represent (v.) to be a symbol or sign of something

amateur (adj.) a person who takes part in a sport for enjoyment, not as a job

scholarship (n.) an amount of money given to someone by an organization to help pay for the person's education

tuition (n.) the money that you pay to be taught, especially in a college or university

spectator sport (n.) a sport that many people watch

iQ RESOURCES Go online to watch the video about sports at Arizona State University. *Resources › Video › Unit 8 › Unit Video*

B. IDENTIFY Watch the video two or three times. Then answer the questions.

1. How many students attend Arizona State?
   _____

2. What sport did Ike Davis play at Arizona State?
   _____

3. What is the average annual cost for a student at Arizona State?
   _____

4. How does Arizona State attract top athletes?
   _____

5. Why do American universities invest in sports?
   _____

C. EXTEND Do you think universities should spend lots of money on sports facilities like stadiums, pools, and golf courses? Why or why not? Write a paragraph of 5–8 sentences in response.

READING 2 199

F. IDENTIFY Look back at Reading 2 to identify the main problem and the solutions. Complete the graphic organizer. Then discuss the questions with a partner.

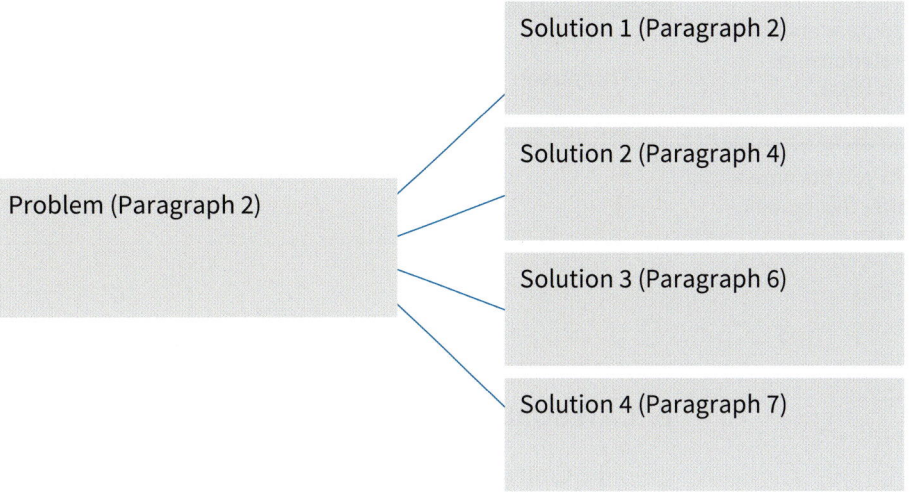

1. Which solution do you think is the best solution? Why?
2. What other solutions can you think of? Are they better solutions than the ones mentioned in the text? Explain.

G. INTERPRET Check (✓) the statements you can infer from the reading.

☐ 1. Overuse injuries are usually permanent.
☐ 2. Fewer children had overuse injuries in the past.
☐ 3. Overuse injuries happen more often to soccer players than baseball players.
☐ 4. It can take children months to recover from an overuse injury.
☐ 5. Parents do not want their children to play casual sports anymore.
☐ 6. It is normal for child athletes to feel sore after they practice sports.
☐ 7. Sharp pain can be a warning sign of an overuse injury.
☐ 8. Young athletes are more at risk of injuring themselves than older athletes are.

H. COMPOSE Why do you think some athletes like to "push through their pain" instead of quitting? Write a paragraph of 5–8 sentences giving your opinion.

I. DISCUSS Discuss the questions in a group. Look back at your Quick Write on page 193 as you think about what you learned.

1. Do you think competing in sports is good for young children? Explain.
2. Do you think coaches and parents have a responsibility to try to stop children from getting hurt while doing sports? Why or why not?

TIP FOR SUCCESS

Activity D asks you to complete a **chart**. A chart is a graphic organizer readers use to see relationships between ideas. Identifying relationships between ideas in a text will help you become a more effective reader.

D. CATEGORIZE Scan Reading 2. Complete the chart with the missing information.

Name	Home	Sport	Injury
1. Courtney Thompson	New Hampshire		
2.		baseball	
3.			sprained ankle, dislocated bone, broken pelvis

E. CATEGORIZE Read the statements. Write *F* (fact) or *O* (opinion).

____ 1. Courtney Thompson practiced gymnastics six days a week.

____ 2. Between 30 and 50 percent of youth sports injuries are due to overuse.

____ 3. Overuse injuries are caused by physical stress on tissue or bone.

____ 4. Child athletes are playing sports too hard for too long.

____ 5. The number of overuse injuries in children is increasing.

____ 6. Soccer player Kevin Butcher showed a lot of dedication.

____ 7. Kevin Butcher's soccer team won the state championship last year.

____ 8. Listening to your body is an important lesson for athletes to learn.

CRITICAL THINKING STRATEGY

Identifying problems and solutions

Writers often **present a problem** as the topic of a reading and then **offer solutions** for the problem. When you read, first identify what the main problem is. Then read through the whole text to find all the solutions.

Next, evaluate the solutions: do you think they solve the problem? What are their disadvantages? Finally, brainstorm alternative solutions to see if there are better ways to solve the problem. Use personal evidence or evidence from the text to justify your opinions.

iQ PRACTICE Go online to watch the Critical Thinking Video and check your comprehension. *Practice > Unit 8 > Activity 8*

4. The official made a **motion** with his hand to let the runners know it was time to start the race.

   a. ticket b. question c. movement

5. Athletes who play sports **aggressively** get hurt more frequently than athletes who don't.

   a. forcefully b. quietly c. quickly

6. Most competitive athletes earn money for playing sports, but gymnasts are an **exception**. They do not receive a salary.

   a. new rule b. someone not included c. professional athlete

7. Competitive athletes must have **dedication** because it takes a lot of time and hard work to be successful in sports.

   a. money b. skill c. commitment

8. Sore, aching muscles are a warning **sign** that you have exercised very hard.

   a. signal b. injury c. sacrifice

9. It can take months for an athlete to **recover** from a serious injury.

   a. compete b. get sick c. get better

iQ PRACTICE Go online for more practice with the vocabulary.
Practice > Unit 8 > Activity 7

C. EXPLAIN Answer the questions. Write the paragraph number where the answer is found. Then discuss your answers with a partner.

1. What are many youth sport injuries due to? Paragraph: ___

2. What causes an overuse injury? Paragraph: ___

3. Why do children in youth sports have more injuries today? Paragraph: ___

4. Why do organized team competitions cause more injuries? Paragraph: ___

5. How can child athletes avoid injury? Paragraph: ___

for two months and needed five months of physical therapy.

◉ Too Much, Too Soon

5   Experts say injuries such as Danny's are on the rise, in part because more and more kids are leaving casual sports for organized team competitions that require hours of practice and game time. "Kids [are] playing sports more **aggressively** at younger ages," explains James Beaty, an orthopedist in Memphis, Tennessee.

6   Kevin Butcher, a 15-year-old soccer player from Fort Collins, Colorado, is no **exception**. He plays soccer three or four times a week for nine months a year. His **dedication** pays off—last year he helped lead his team to a state championship. But his success came with a price. "Last year, I sprained my ankle a few times, dislocated[3] a bone in my foot, and broke both sides of my pelvis[4]," Kevin says. The first time he broke his pelvis, Kevin didn't realize it for about a month. He played through the pain until doctors forced him to rest. When he dislocated a bone in his foot, a physical therapist put the bone into place, bandaged his foot, and let him play the next day.

◉ Knowing Your Limits

7   Not every kid who plays sports ends up with serious injuries. Experts say the key to avoiding injury is paying attention to your body. Feeling sore after practice is OK, but sharp pain is a warning **sign** that shouldn't be ignored. Kevin learned that lesson while **recovering** from his second broken pelvis in less than a year. "There's definitely a glory in playing through pain, but I think there is a limit. You just have to know when to stop."

[3] **dislocate:** to put a bone out of its correct position
[4] **pelvis:** the set of wide bones at the bottom of your back that connect to your legs

---

VOCABULARY SKILL REVIEW

In Unit 4, you learned how to identify word forms with suffixes. Which of the vocabulary words in Activity B have a suffix making them a noun?

B. VOCABULARY Here are some words from Reading 2. Read the sentences. Circle the word or phrase that can replace the bold word without changing the meaning. Then compare your answers with a partner.

1. Ice skating is a **demanding** sport that requires a lot of time, practice, and hard work.

   a. difficult   b. expensive   c. harmful

2. Putting kids in sports at a young age is a growing **trend** in many countries today.

   a. new profession   b. general change   c. high cost

3. We canceled the soccer game **due to** the pouring rain. It was too wet and dangerous to play.

   a. because of   b. in order to   c. late for